D0404167

PENGUINS & GOLDEN CALVES

PENTICTON UNITED CHURCH
LIBRARY

By Madeleine L'Engle

An Acceptable Time

And Both Were Young

And It Was Good

The Anti-Muffins

Anytime Prayers

The Arm of the Starfish

Camilla

Certain Women

A Circle of Quiet

A Cry Like a Bell

Dance in the Desert

Dragons in the Waters

Everyday Prayers

The Glorious Impossible

A House Like a Lotus

Ilsa

The Irrational Season

The Journey with Jonah

Ladder of Angels

Lines Scribbled on an Envelope

Love Letters

Many Waters

Meet the Austins

The Moon by Night

The Other Side of the Sun

Prayers for Sunday

A Ring of Endless Light

The Rock That Is Higher

A Severed Wasp

The Small Rain

Sold into Egypt

The Sphinx at Dawn

A Stone for a Pillow

The Summer of the
   Great-Grandmother

A Swiftly Tilting Planet

Trailing Clouds of Glory

Troubling a Star

The Twenty-four Days Before
   Christmas

Two-Part Invention

Walking on Water

The Weather of the Heart

A Wind in the Door

A Winter's Love

A Wrinkle in Time

The Young Unicorns

PENGUINS ✛ GOLDEN CALVES

icons and idols

MADELEINE L'ENGLE

Northstone

© 1996 by Crosswicks, Inc.

Published in Canada by Northstone Press by arrangement with Harold Shaw Publishers.

All rights reserved. No part of this book may be reproduced or transmitted in any form or by any means, electronic or mechanical, including photocopying, recording, or any information storage and retrieval system without written permission from Harold Shaw Publishers, Box 567, Wheaton, Illinois 60189. Printed in the United States of America.

Northstone Publishing, Inc., is an employee-owned company, committed to caring for the environment and all creation. Northstone recycles, reuses and composts, and encourages readers to do the same. Resources are printed on recycled paper and more environmentally friendly groundwood papers (newsprint) whenever possible. The trees used are replaced through donations to the Scoutrees for Canada Program. Ten percent of all profit is donated to charitable organizations.

All Scripture quotations, unless otherwise indicated, are taken from The Holy Bible, King James Version.

Canadian Cataloguing in Publication Data
   A catalogue record for this publication is available from the National Library of Canada.

03 02 01 00 99 98 97

10 9 8 7 6 5 4 3 2 1

Northstone

To Barbara and Bob Tarr
with thanks for their hospitality
which has given me time and place to write

Contents

I

A CALF IN HOREB

It can't be done.

It's impossible.

Words are not adequate to describe the raw and violent beauty of the bottom of the world, the land and frozen waters of the Antarctic continent.

"Where did you say you were going?" I was asked.

"Antarctica."

"Are you crazy?" The questioner did not say, "At your age,"—seventy-four at the time—but the question was implied.

"Probably."

"But why on earth . . . Antarctica?"

"I thought I'd better go while I'm still able to get in and out of zodiacs."

The questioner looked even more dubious. Zodiacs are small inflatable rubber boats. "Well," I explained, "all our shore excursions will be by zodiac."

"But where do you stay at night? In hotels?"

I smiled. "There are no hotels. We'll stay on our boat." Our home away from home on this journey was to be a small ship which would take us from the southernmost parts of Chile to Antarctica.

Maybe I am crazy, I thought. Why am I going so far away? Why would anybody want to go to the frozen wastes of Antarctica? I was going largely because my son and my daughter-in-law and I had been talking about and planning this excursion for two years. Perhaps I was not in the best position to make such a trek at that moment in time, since I was not quite six months away from the automobile accident that nearly took my life. But I knew if I didn't go then I wouldn't go at all. The plans couldn't be postponed.

I had, in fact, canceled my part of the trip.

Then my son said, "It was a lovely dream, Mother, but if you don't go, we don't go."

Emotional blackmail?

I put my name back on the passenger list. Anyhow, was New York that much safer than Antarctica? Was any place? Certainly San Diego was not, where a careless truck driver had run a red light. Is safety what I am looking for? Is God any further away as I'm whizzed through ice floes than when I cross Amsterdam Avenue and 110th Street in New York?

In mid-January we started on the long journey, and it was long! That's one thing that protects Antarctica from too much tourism. First we flew to Miami. Then came a long, overnight flight to Santiago, Chile, where we stayed for two days in sweltering heat, hardly able to believe that we would shortly be seeing icebergs and glaciers.

Two more planes brought us to Punta Arenas, Chile, where we boarded our small ship, known as "the little red boat," and *little* was the operative word.

It was several days before the almost balmy weather turned cold, clear, with bitter winds. Katabatic winds, they are called. Then we began to see ice floes. And glaciers, and "mountains of the moon," making us feel that we were sailing back in time as well as space. This is what the planet looked like during the Ice Age. Clean. Pure. Ruthless.

As much as possible we had read up on the Antarctic continent and its history before leaving, had followed on maps the trails of the early explorers trying to reach the South Pole. We had read about penguins and seals and the great whales, and about the albatross which has the longest wing span of any bird, so that it can sail the winds as the old winged ships sailed the seas.

Even so, I was not prepared for my first encounter with penguins. We set off in our little black zodiacs, zooming towards land, looking across the open water to icebergs, glaciers, stone mountains stark and barren, mountains scoured by the wild wind and waters of the planet as it was being formed. The air is clear and dryer than the Sahara Desert. No snow has fallen on the great Antarctic icecap for billions of years. In the surrounding ocean the majestic icebergs glow with an incredibly intense blue light. My son reminded me that I have now been to all seven continents. This one staggered me with its uniqueness. I felt as though I was on one of the outer planets, far from the parent sun.

Suddenly an unexpected smell assailed our nostrils. We sniffed. Our guide laughed and told us that we were smelling penguin guano. "You smell them before you hear or see them."

It was not a vile smell, because there was nothing about it of decay or corruption. But we certainly didn't want to bottle it and take it home! As our little zodiac approached the shore we smelled, heard, and saw the penguins in that order. They were Rock Hopper penguins, small, about three feet tall, noisy, funny, waddling at an amazing pace, or simply hopping from the beach up onto the rocks.

We had been warned not to interfere in any way with the penguins, not to get closer than fifteen feet to any of these birds, and never to block their route from the land to the sea. But the penguins had not heard that request, and they came rushing towards our group. We may have looked like great red birds to them, all of us in our regulation red parkas which would not only keep us warm, but would also make us visible if we should stray from the group, something we were strenuously warned not to do.

Penguins, one of our lecturers told us, never do anything alone. The penguin is a completely communal creature. There is no equivalent of a solitary blue heron in the penguin world. When one heads for the sea, two or three will follow. The baby penguins huddle together in what are called crêches. There is safety in numbers. While they are young and still unable to swim, the little ones are extremely vulnerable to predators, especially a large, brown raptor bird called a skua. When they are older they fall prey to seals: leopard seals, fur seals. They tend to stick together for safety's sake. But despite their communal nature, they know no intimacy. Intimacy is dangerous. If you open your heart to a mate or a chick and in the next hour that mate or chick gets eaten, you open yourself to loss and grief.

It so happened that shortly before leaving for Antarctica I had read an article about intimacy between parents and children in a so-called primitive tribe: now that modern medicine has insured that most babies will live, the parents are allowing themselves an intimacy with their offspring that had not been possible when many babies died in infancy or early childhood.

And I remembered going with my mother to a beautiful southern graveyard where many of my forebears, including my father, were buried. What struck deepest at my heart was the repeated sight of four or even five little tombstones in a row, four or five children in one family after another, wiped out in a few days by scarlet fever or diphtheria. Because of antibiotics, we no longer fear scarlet fever or diphtheria. But I remembered one of my southern cousins, my mother's age, saying that scarlet fever had killed five of her brothers and sisters in a week. And I wondered how the parents and the remaining siblings survived such multiple grief. Did parents hold back from intimacy until the children had survived those early, precarious years? How did a woman feel, knowing that if she had eight or ten or twelve children she'd be lucky if she raised half of them?

Now that the death of a little one is not the norm, it has become unusual and terrible. Is there any way a woman can nurse a baby and not feel intimacy? Was that why wet nurses used to be employed? And, later, why bottles of formula were substituted for the mother's breast—to prevent an intimacy that could be shattered by illness and death? I nursed my babies; nursing is as intimate an act as making love.

And then I thought: perhaps the very precariousness of human relations made the intimacy all the more poignant and all the more treasured. It's only been in the past few generations that we have been allowed easy intimacy, assuming that mothers will not die in childbirth, that babies will live to have babies themselves, that we'll all reach retirement age and enjoy our well-earned leisure. Perhaps that's why we've messed up intimacy; we simply weren't prepared for a lifetime of intimacy—and still aren't.

How much are we supposed to protect ourselves by holding back from intimacy? Isn't the easy, instant, pseudo-intimacy, which is all that many people know, one of the best protections against real intimacy? A TV or radio interviewer jumps immediately into using first names and asks personal questions on the air which would have been unthinkable only a few decades ago. But the intimacy is fake; the interviewer and interviewee will probably never see each other again. True intimacy takes time, is built up over days, months, years. Two of my deepest friendships go back to the teens. Over the years I have met people and I have thought, Yes! There is potential for real friendship here, for intimacy. But it has of necessity taken time, a willingness to share, risk, be vulnerable, understand idiosyncrasies, allow for flaws. And suddenly, rejoicing in friendship, I realize that I have known so-and-so for over ten years. It does take time. It is worth it. More than worth it.

And words cannot describe it. Nor can words describe what the funny little Rock Hoppers were teaching me about vulnerability.

I watched one of them head down a frozen dune to the shore, immediately followed by three other penguins. They have fun. They play. They throw themselves into the water. Suddenly I understood that the penguin flies in the water and waddles on land. The penguin is a bird, but the penguin's natural element is the sea.

What is the natural element for us mortals? Did we lose it when we left Eden? Are we losing even more of it as we try to protect ourselves from any kind of pain, inner or outer? Perhaps one price we must be willing to pay in order to be what we call "human" is to be vulnerable. To love each other. To be willing, if necessary, to die for each other. To let each other die when the time comes. So the penguin, lacking intimacy by its very nature, became for me an icon, an icon of vulnerability.

What do I mean by icon?

If it's impossible for me to describe the wild wonderfulness of Antarctica, it is equally impossible for me to describe what I, personally, mean by icon. I am not thinking of the classic definition of the icons so familiar in the orthodox church, icons of Christ, the Theotokos, saints, painted on wood and often partially covered with silver. My personal definition is much wider, and the simplest way I can put it into words is to affirm that an icon, for me, is an open window to God. An icon is something I can look through and get a wider glimpse of God and God's demands on us, el's mortal children, than I would otherwise. It is not flippant for me to say that a penguin is an icon for me, because the penguin invited me to look through its odd little self and on to a God who demands of us that we be vulnerable as we open ourselves to intimacy, an intimacy which leads not only to love of creature, but to love of God.

I have some icons that are more traditional. On the night stand in my cabin I placed a small travel copy of the famous icon of Abraham's three angelic guests, three beautiful, winged angels, who are also, understood iconically, Father, Son, and Holy Spirit. It is what we think of as a classic icon, saying something that cannot be said in words, that cannot even be said in the painting. It transcends our experience and points us to something larger and greater and more wonderful. Yes, it is an open window to God.

But a penguin for an icon?

Why not? When I look around the ancient, ice-bound world of the penguin, I am totally aware of Creation, of the majesty and glory of what the Maker has wrought, in a part of the planet still unsullied by us thoughtless, careless mortals. And I am reminded once again that just as words are inadequate to describe the icy beauty around me, so are words inadequate to describe the Maker's love for me, and I, the made, to describe my love of the Maker. I need icons, and

I find them everywhere even if, like the penguin, they are anything but traditional!

Unlike some of the great birds who mate for life, the penguin does not. If, at mating time, last year's mate appears, well and good. If not, another mate will do. The change does not seem terribly important. What is important is two penguins getting together so that eggs can be laid, chicks be hatched.

It's not like that for us. At least, not for me. I mated for life and was blessed that my husband did, also. Our love made us both vulnerable. Hugh's death was a tearing of my life in half. But would I want to be invulnerable? I don't think so. It may be my very vulnerability that accents my need for icons.

I am a storyteller, and I need icons. But not in the sense that the word *icon* is now being used in secular terms. On a radio commercial a certain magazine was referred to as being an icon. It was not a theological or religious magazine, but a totally secular one, full of juicy gossip. An icon? If something does not lead us to God it is not and cannot be an icon. In the computer program Windows, the word *icon* is used again, as a symbol for a graphic element. No, no! If an icon is not a window to God it is not an icon! Let us not be confused!

True icons reveal more of God to me than I have hitherto understood. The classic icon, usually painted on wood, opens a window for me. One of my favorites is of King David sitting on his royal throne. With one arm he is holding his golden harp. With the other he is holding the Christ child, who is sitting on his lap. This is not anachronistic! Chronology explodes! I am thrust into God's time.

True story is also an icon for me. Storytellers try to say something that is beyond the words of the story, that takes us further than mere facts. Jesus taught by telling stories. Stories are icons for me.

In *A Circle of Quiet* I wrote, "If an image is not easy to define, an icon is even more difficult. We usually think of icons as corrupt images which ought to be broken. But it is only the icon misused which needs breaking. A true icon is not a reflection; it is a metaphor, a different, unlike look at something, and carries within it something of that at which it looks."

In *Walking on Water* I tried again: "An icon is a symbol, rather than a sign. A sign may point the way to something, such as 'Athens—10 kilometers.' But the sign is not Athens, even when we reach the city limits and read 'Athens.' A symbol, however, unlike a sign, contains within it some quality of what it represents. An icon of the Annunciation, for instance, does more than point to the angel and the girl; it contains, for us, some of Mary's acceptance and obedience, and so affects our own ability to accept, to obey."

Not everybody needs icons. For some Christians the way of negation works more truly than the way of affirmation: since it is impossible for a mortal to define God in any way, all symbols are to be avoided.

For those of us who choose the way of affirmation it is equally evident that anything we can say or show about God is inadequate, but nevertheless an icon can be an open door, or window, to God.

An icon is beyond simile. A simile tries to tell us something more than the facts. *Like* has been weakened as a simile word by constant misuse: "I said . . . Like I can't find my blue jeans" We hear *like* misused constantly, but it's still a useful word, our simile word, our word for something we can't quite describe so we reach for something *like* it. "I can't tell you what it is, but it's something like this." "My love is like a red, red rose." "This night is unlike any other night." "This piece of meat is like leather."

An icon is more than a simile; it is a metaphor, containing within itself something of the indescribable, so that the need for description vanishes. It is not just *like*. *It is.* Jesus is God. What an affirmation! Jesus is not *like* God, Jesus *is* God, the ultimate metaphor. Poets use both similes and metaphors, but metaphor is the stronger. "The moon is a golden galleon." "My love is the sun and the moon."

Whatever is an open door to God is, for me, an icon. It may be that small picture pasted on wood with which I travel. The icon of the three angels, the Holy Trinity, does not prove to me anything about God, but it opens the doors and windows of my heart.

As long as my icons remain icons for me I am able to accept their truth as far beyond our mortal mind's capacity for conception. But we try, anyhow, to use inadequate words to express what we feel about the universe in which we live, and our love for the One who made it.

Our need for icons begins in early childhood when we hold on to the favourite little piece of blanket, or the beloved stuffed animal. The blanket is not a blanket, nor is the animal a mere animal; they are icons of all-rightness in a world that early shows itself to be not all right. They are icons of tender love in a society that daily becomes more brutal and violent.

The blanket gradually gets smaller and smaller from the fondling of little hands until finally it vanishes—usually at the time when the child is ready to give it up. The stuffed animal ultimately sits on the bookshelf, nearly forgotten, and this is right and proper; the child has outgrown the need for this particular icon. In the attic bedroom at Crosswicks, our old house in the country, a goodly number of stuffed animals remain in various stages of batterdom. The grown children no longer need them, but neither do they want them to be given away. And that, too, is good. They are icons, not idols.

The psalmist warns us about idols: "They have eyes and see not, ears and hear not, hands and handle not." And, furthermore, the psalmist tells us that those who turn to idols become like their idols. The fear of idolatry is behind the Hebrew lack of graphic art.

But it's not only a Hebrew fear. It has influenced a large part of Christendom, also, and it springs from a misunderstanding of the first commandment: "Thou shalt not make unto thee any graven image, or any likeness of any thing that is in heaven above, or that is in the earth beneath, or that is in the water under the earth."

And many people stop there. But the commandment goes on to say: "Thou shalt not bow down thyself to them, nor serve them." In that sentence lies the meaning of the commandment. You may not turn an image into God, because that is to turn an icon into an idol. It is not that we need iconoclasts; we need idoloclasts.

So, even if we understand that praying through icons is not idolatry, why do we mortals need icons? Icons are not adequate, nor are sunset and moonrise and starfilled skies, though they are icons of God's creation. Perhaps we need icons because of the very inadequacy of our ability to understand God. A friend sent me a small card which reads, A COMPREHENDED GOD IS NO GOD. We can love God, but we mortals cannot understand the nature of the infinite Creator, and so we turn to icons.

For those of us who have a strong sense of our need for icons, the discoveries of science are not to be feared. All they can do is show us a universe even more glorious, marvelous, and complex than we could have dreamed. The mighty Word which called all things into being is also the Infinite God and cannot be completely known by the finite creature. We are given glimpses, epiphanies, when the boundaries of time and space are broken. And we are given icons; icons which illuminate God's love for us in a living and creative way.

Too often we are tempted to turn and worship the icon, and that is idolatry. The golden calf of the Israelites in the wilderness is the prototypical idol, the man-made creature which was worshiped instead of the Creator, dead metal rather than Living Maker.

After the flight from Egypt, the amazing journey through the Red Sea, the long years of trekking towards the Promised Land, Moses was over-long talking with God, and the impatient and anxious people felt abandoned both by Moses and God. They said to Aaron, "Up, make us gods, which shall go before us; as for this Moses, the man that brought us up out of the land of Egypt, we know not what is become of him."

And Aaron (what was he thinking of? We would have expected better of him!) said unto them, "Break off the golden earrings, which are in the ears of your wives, and of your sons, and of your daughters, and bring them unto me." And Aaron melted down all the jewelry which was given him and made a golden calf, and "He built an altar before it."

Aaron and the people did what God had clearly forbidden: "They made a calf in Horeb, and worshiped the molten image. Thus they turned their glory into the similitude of a calf that eats hay." They tried to turn their idol into a god and of course it did not work; it never does.

And Moses, coming down from the mountain after talking with God, saw the golden calf and the people dancing around it, and he was furious, and told Aaron so in no uncertain terms. Aaron defended himself, explaining that the people wanted gods to go with them, and they didn't know where Moses was, so Aaron took their gold, and threw it into the fire, and "Out came this calf"! Rationalizing and alibi-ing, just as we still do today: Who, me? I had nothing to do with it. Out came this calf!

An icon does not have to be an idol. An icon should give us glimpses of our God who is both immanent and transcendent, knowable and unknowable. If an icon becomes more important to us than what it reveals of God, then it becomes a golden calf, but this does not need to happen.

In my prayer corner at home are several icons which have been given to me and thus are doubly iconic; they represent the love of the giver as well as the subject of the icon. I do not love these icons as things-in-themselves. They are not idols. I do not worship them. I could lose one of them, give it away, have it stolen, and it would remain a real icon for me. It is not the painting on wood that is the icon, but what that painting on wood leads me to in my human attempts to love my Creator.

Enough! Enough! All my words do no more than point out their inadequacy.

Jesus, of course, is the perfect icon of intimacy; God, being so willing to show us how to love that the Maker of the Galaxies became totally intimate with a particular human body, became one of us. What greater intimacy could there be?

Jesus had intimate friends, all of whom betrayed him, but he did not hold himself back from intimacy, and he must have known how easily that intimacy could be betrayed. When his closest friends did not understand him, when all the disciples abandoned him in the garden, that may have been a far worse pain than the pain of crucifixion. But he responded not with anger but with forgiveness and compassion. After his resurrection, when he returned to his disciples and friends, he bestowed peace upon them, not anger or punishment. The first thing he said to them was not, "Where were you when I needed you?" but, "Peace be with you."

Jesus was vulnerable not only with John and James and Peter, but with Mary of Magdala and Mary and Martha of Bethany, and with all his friends. He made himself vulnerable to the religious institution of his day, an institution which was very dear to him. Yet the institution not only did not understand him, it crucified him. Alas, institutions often become idolatrous in their efforts to protect and preserve themselves. Institutions do not like being vulnerable.

When we make ourselves vulnerable, we do open ourselves to pain, sometimes excruciating pain. The more people we love, the more we are liable to be hurt, and not only by the people we love, but for the people we love. When anyone I love is in pain—physical, mental, spiritual—I, too, am in pain. There has been a lot of pain this past year. It has not been a good year for the world, and it has not been a good year for many people who are dear to me. But our souls do not grow if we insulate ourselves from pain.

One of the most widely used defenses against intimacy throughout the centuries is domination. Power. Control. A world of domination is poignantly illustrated for us in much of Scripture and in much of Christendom. Is Protestant fear of Catholicism fear of the power of Rome? When one branch of Christendom denounces another, is not power at least part of the motive? Why are Christians no longer known by how they love one another, but rather by how they vilify and sometimes hate each other? Why do some popular preachers suddenly become drunk with power? When we wield power over other people, are we not becoming idolatrous as we take over the prerogatives of God?

Doctors and nurses seem to assume power over their patients by immediately calling them by their first names. Parents have complete power over their children. Some parents believe that if they love their children, they will chastise them with the whip, or beat them into submission. It is horrifying that people look for and find justification for this in Scripture. Power is a denial of intimacy.

I did not want to dominate my little ones. I wanted intimacy. Of course, when they were infants I had the potential for power. Human babies are the only creatures born totally helpless. It would seem that a baby is born still in the fetal stage, so that its head will not grow so large that it will tear the mother to bits during birth. A wailing, colicky baby can drive a mother nearly distracted. I was blessed in having healthy babies whose hunger for my milk was reasonably spaced through day and night, who slept through the night when they were three months old. It wasn't that difficult for me to learn a nurturing intimacy, but I cannot but help having sympathy for the mother who loses control after weeks or months of sleepless nights and a constantly screaming infant. Still, despite the fact that we have total power over these little ones, true intimacy demands patience, laughter, and forgiveness—as much of ourselves as of our babies.

Later on, as they begin to walk, talk, discover, want their own way, intimacy still demands a calm willingness to show the child what is creative and what is disruptive to the family. Much of this has to be done by the example of the parents. There's the rub.

What about the domination of the wife by the husband? That was taken for granted until well into this century. Two of my godmother's great aunts were named Patience and Submit. Women were possessions. Men felt that they had the right to beat their wives, because their wives were their property, and the husband exercised what were called "conjugal rights." Although there must have been a deep love and partnership in some marriages, in many marriages women were simply there for the use of their husbands, and nice women were not supposed to enjoy sex. Good women were supposed to give their husbands progeny, particularly male progeny, but they weren't supposed to enjoy it. Enjoyment was only for those women Scripture sometimes calls "whores of Babylon."

At marriage anything that the wife had—money, real estate, jewelry, whatever—became the man's property. A woman's value was defined by her mate. An unmarried woman was regarded as useless and discarded by society. One reason Jesus was so adamant about the sanctity of marriage was that two thousand years ago a man could say to his wife, "I divorce you, I divorce you, I divorce you," and get rid of her in a moment, leaving her with nothing. For some of these rejected women there was no way to live except by prostitution. Jesus, in terms of his own day, was trying to protect women from such abuse.

This is not the place to get into the argument, pro or con, about contraceptives, but my paternal grandmother had a baby regularly every year. One year after the birth of one child she prayed, "Dear Lord, please, please, let me go two years without a baby." Two years to the day she had twins.

I'm not sure whose sense of humor this was. She certainly did not think it funny.

My maternal grandmother had three pregnancies, four children: my mother, twin boys, and another little boy. When the children were grown and her marriage broken, my grandmother moved into what in those days would have been called "good works." At the beach near her southern town there were many drownings; she started a life-saving corps. Many strangers passed through the town, arriving at or leaving from the great, neo-Greek railroad station; she set up a Travelers' Aid station. She fought for the vote, for other women's rights—though in those days these probably wouldn't have been called "good works."

I was not as intimate with either of my grandmothers as my granddaughters are with me, because I did not see much of them. My paternal grandmother died when I was three, and my strongest memory of her is of sitting in her lap in a big old rocking chair. On the table beside us was a lamp with a sunny yellow china shade; it still lights my desk. It's a warm memory, an intimate memory.

I saw my maternal grandmother a little more, but not a great deal—a trip south once a year. I particularly remember her garden, which seemed exotic to this New York City girl and was her pride and joy. Many plants were carefully nurtured in her greenhouse before being taken outdoors. At the bottom of the garden was a thick, protective wall of bamboo. There was a great fig tree which bore delicious fruit. Mocking birds sang. When there was snow in New York the sun was warm in her garden. Sometimes I was allowed to sleep on the screened-in sleeping porch off her bedroom, where I was surrounded by green and by bird song. Best of all were glorious visits to her cottage at the beach, where my memories are far more of place than of person, dunes topped with waving golden sea oats and the dark vines of scuppernong grapes. Above all, the ocean, the sound of the breakers, was always in our ears. In the morning when I woke up I could see moving light flickering across my ceiling, the reflection of the early sun on the water.

Her lap, too, provides a memory of intimacy, of sitting on the porch of the cottage in a big green rocking chair and being rocked and sung to, "Jesus, tender shepherd . . . "

The world she grew up in was completely different from mine. I was born into a world where I could reasonably hope for a good education and enough mathematical ability (in my case, barely) to open my own bank account, keep my own cheque book. I could, at the appropriate age, vote and take the job for which I had equipped myself.

This was certainly not true for my mother or my grandmothers. Small, sanitary helps that I take for granted did not exist for them. When did toilet paper come in? Sanitary pads? My mother told me how old sheets were saved, cut up in strips, used monthly, washed out and saved for the next month. Women were just beginning to be accepted at colleges, women's colleges. They were not welcome in men's colleges, and the few women who made it through medical school or law school had to have immense patience and persistence and stubbornness in the face of resistance, rejection, rudeness. One young friend of mine, who did her internship only a few decades ago, said that the male doctors enjoyed telling filthy jokes in front of her in order to embarrass her.

Intimacy between friends involves a nondominant love, as well as vulnerability. With a true friend we can share the deepest places of our hearts, the dark as well as the light. I have friends whose secrets will go to the grave with me, as mine with them. We listen, we share, we laugh, we accept. We seldom give advice, and when we do it is for love, not power. We play together, and this is a special delight for me in my mid-seventies, to have friends with whom I can play with the enthusiasm and whole-heartedness of a child.

A friend said to me, "Madeleine, you should see your face when you play Ping-Pong."

I looked at her questioningly.

"You look just like a child."

Perhaps I do play Ping-Pong like a child, but that's half the fun, running several yards in order to slam a serve, leaping after the ball, laughing in delight as a wild shot works. My friend should see her own face when she plays Ping-Pong! We're very well matched and we play hard, and we work up a sweat and laugh a lot and have fun.

Sometimes after dinner with friends we play charades, and this is as much fun now as it was when I was a kid. Last winter in Honolulu a ten-year-old boy gave me a set of jacks, real jacks, the heavy, old fashioned, metal ones. I'm not as good a jacks player as I used to be, but given a little more practise . . . .

Play is part of intimacy, and in our busy world we don't play enough.

A friend who over the years has become an intimate friend shared with me this quotation of Georgia O'Keeffe:

> A flower is relatively small. Everyone has many associations with a flower—the idea of flowers. You put out your hand to touch the flower—lean forward to smell it—maybe touch it with your lips almost without thinking—or give it to someone to please them. Still—in a way—nobody sees a flower—really—it is so small—we haven't time—and to see takes time, like having a friend takes time.

2

FALSE EXPECTATIONS

 When I went to Antarctica I went with a sense of mystery, of not knowing in any definitive way what I was going to see. Granted, we'd read books, seen videos, looked at pictures, but we knew that these gave us only a faint idea of what we would actually experience.

Penguins, for instance. The pictures give one little idea of their relative sizes. The Rock Hoppers, the first penguins we saw, were smaller than I had expected, no more than two or three feet tall. The King penguins were nearly twice their size, and Emperors are even larger. The different species have varying head dresses, feathers sticking up, smooth heads, top knots—there are a lot of individual differences. I'd thought a penguin was a penguin was a penguin. That was just as silly as thinking all White people—or Black people—or Yellow people—look alike. We often have expectations that are not so much false as inadequate. Now I am told that it is not politically correct to refer to people by color "because it's pejorative." Is it? Why? I am not told why, but the correct phrasing is Caucasian, African, or Asian. And why Caucasian? As far as I know, very few of my forebears came from anywhere near the Caucasus.

It is not the adjective but the way we use it that makes it pejorative. When we use words to put down, to divide, we are falling into idolatry. My childhood book of Bible stories made clear that the three wise men were White, Black, and Yellow, emphasizing that all races on earth were included; no one was left out. Not one of the kings was wiser, or better looking, or more richly endowed than another. It was only as I grew up that I began to understand racism, and how one race can look down on another, be ill-treated by another, thought to be less loved by God than another. I learned it with anguish, graduating from college right into the Second World War.

It made us think, that war; and some of the best thinking came from our artists. *South Pacific*, the beautiful musical play about some aspects of that war, contains the lovely song "You've Got to Be Carefully Taught." We need to be taught to hate people of a different color, or religion, or language. This is not innate in children, who rejoice over differences until they are taught to fear them.

Being taught to fear differences goes along with false expectations. What will the neighbors think? What will the Joneses say? Don't do that, or people will look down on you. Don't be different. Conform.

We mortals frequently stumble over false expectations, and I wonder if there were always as many as there are today. TV commercials try to persuade us that we are entitled to glamour which will never fade with age as long as we use the correct creams and lotions; that there are pills to take away all pain; that love should forever be romantic; that if we buy the right drugs and pay our insurance premiums we will live forever, a life of affluence, superficiality, and material possessions.

False expectations = golden calves.

Recently someone said to me, "I just want life to be normal."

And I asked her, "What's normal?" We've fallen for the lie that normal means easy and placid, with no problems, and that's not normal at all. But all kinds of false expectations have slipped into our lives, and I'm prone to them, too.

For instance, I want ordained clergy, both men and women, to keep impossibly high standards. I do believe that if we have high expectations of people they are more likely to rise to them than if we cynically expect them to lead subverted, immoral lives. But the over-high expectations can be crippling, too. I want doctors to know more than I should expect them to know; after all, they are only creatures like me who have had a lot more education in an area where I am largely ignorant. Most of us share, at least to some extent, these false expectations.

Since I spent my early post-college years working in the theatre, I resent the assumption that all actors are totally self-centered, that they run around having casual affairs and are affected and unreal. I met many people while I was working in the theatre who led Christ-centered lives, who taught me a great deal about standards, about love. I even married one of them!

I don't like compartmentalization: All actors are . . . All New Yorkers are . . . All artists are . . . All Christians are. . .

Recently I heard a story about a man who was talking about the current problems of sex to his teen age son. The boy asked him, "Dad, tell me, how have you practised safe sex?" The father answered, "With a wedding ring."

False expectations are all over and have seeped into our religious holy days. What have we come to expect about Christmas? Why are there more suicides at this time of year than any other? Why are people so lonely and despairing that they prefer death to life during this, the greatest affirmation of life the human being has ever been given? What have we done to Christmas?

We have our beloved family gatherings, but there are also office parties. During the Christmas season I receive more invitations than usual to cocktail parties. My husband felt the same way about both coffee hours and cocktail parties: that they defeat the purpose of bringing people together in a friendly way and emphasize the loneliness of anyone on the fringe. The person you are talking to is frequently looking over your shoulder to see if there's somebody more important he should be talking to. But it doesn't have to be this way! Two parishioners at my church offered to cook a seated Christmas dinner (in our Parish Hall, which is about as attractive as most parish halls) for anybody who wanted to come. Nearly a hundred people were there, creating family, which is one of the jobs of the body of Christ. One of the most important callings of a parish family is to see that nobody drops through the cracks at holiday time.

But what has happened to our observance of Christmas itself? Over the centuries we've sentimentalized it to the point where we have almost entirely forgotten the incredible love of God in leaving heaven and coming to us as an unthinking zygote in the womb of a young girl. It boggles our limited imaginations! The sacrifice that the all-powerful God made in limiting that power to our mortality is too potent for our fragile "belief systems." It's beyond us, and so we've managed to water it down. The Christmas Pageant which, I believe, should include the entire congregation, is given by the children, so we can wax more and more sentimental at their cuteness.

One year at my church Mary was played by a young woman in her eighth month of pregnancy. The Baby Jesus was a three-week-old little boy. Our three kings were, as tradition calls them to be, Black, White, and Yellow. (Whoops, African, Caucasian, and Asian. Or should it be Indo-European, African, Asian?) Herod was one of our young actor members, and his soldiers were teenage boys. The angel Gabriel was played by one of our professional dancers. The Gospel accounts were read by an articulate teenager. The baby angels of course evoked coos of appreciation. The whole parish was involved, and that, for me, helped move the story of the birth of the Lord Jesus from sentimentality into glorious reality.

Almost all our holy days have suffered from what we have done to them, some almost entirely losing their original meaning. Many years ago on All Hallow's Eve I was in boarding school, and one of my friends came up to me. "Hey, Madeleine, there's a letter for you in your box." I hadn't been expecting a letter, so I went to see what it was. It was from my mother, briefly telling me that my father was in the hospital with pneumonia, and ending, "Pray for us."

This was shortly before the discovery of penicillin, and my father's lungs had been gassed in the First World War. I knew the outlook was grim. My father's coughing had been a part of my entire life. I still found it hard to accept that now he was dying.

I was summoned to the headmistress's office and told that I was to take the train home. But I had to go to study hall first, for an hour or so.

The study hall was in a basement room where there were windows halfway up the wall that opened onto the street. While we were doing homework, groups of little boys with wildly painted Hallowe'en faces peered through the windows at us, shouting and laughing. To me it sounded like screaming.

It is that image of Hallowe'en which is forever printed on my memory's retina.

Two of the teachers drove me to the train station, gauchely silent, not knowing what to say to me. I had picked up a book to read on the train, *Jane Eyre*. Perhaps I thought the old, familiar story of Jane's woes would help me keep my anxiety under control. I wanted to pray, but the old childish prayers didn't work. The wheels clacked along the tracks in a steady rhythm, and with that beat I found myself repeating, over and over, "Dear God, please do whatever is best for Father, please do whatever is best for Father." (Ever since it has been my most frequent intercessory prayer, no matter who I am praying for.) By the time I got home my father was dead.

This was not my first experience of death, but it was the first when I was truly out of childhood, which is perhaps why I have needed to write about it more than once. I was seventeen. All I had been taught about death was that it was important to be brave. As a society we were not good about death then; we are not good about death now.

Hallowe'en, the evening of All Hallow's, that eve when we contemplate those who have gone before us, used to be a lovely and hopeful part of our story. What has happened to it? Why have we turned it into an ugly golden calf? As far as I know, America is the only country that has secularized and made blasphemous a day that was meant to be holy and quiet and contemplative. In many places in Europe it is still celebrated as All Hallow's Eve, the time when those who have died are remembered with love and prayers, and where we count on that great cloud of witnesses to pray for us. It is an old, old tradition, going back in human time to the centuries before Jesus, when the great harvest feast of Samhain was celebrated, and a great thanksgiving banquet was held with places set for those who had died during the year. It was also understood that the spirits of the longer dead would stand behind the chairs with their benign presence, giving their blessing to the living and assuring us that our lives have meaning which will not be lost but will continue after our deaths.

What has happened?

Hallowe'en in my part of the world comes at the turn of the year when the trees are being stripped of their leaves; when the sap runs more and more slowly, preparing for the long death of winter, and the rebirth of spring. The season itself is a time when our thoughts turn to the mysteries of life and death. It is a time when I always think of my father, and that in the great scheme of things his life, as all life, mattered. His very matter mattered. *Matter matters.*

My belief that matter matters is tied in with my understanding of the Incarnation. Yes! The magnificent energy of Christ took on matter, and all for love of us mortals, thereby dignifying matter forever.

How on earth did the idea ever sneak into our thinking that matter, the flesh, is evil, while only the spirit is good? What a horrendous mistake, which has distorted our understanding of the Incarnation ever since!

It reminds me of a time when a computer was programmed to translate English into Russian, and vice versa. The phrase "the spirit is willing, but the flesh is weak" was fed into the computer and translated into Russian. It then was decided to feed the Russian into the computer and get the original back. What came out was, "The wine is good here, but the meat is tough."

We've done the equivalent of feeding our Christian faith in and out of computers until we fall for faulty translations and forget the incredible action of Love in the Mystery of the Word Made Flesh.

It is mystery. What we believe is mystery, as our very being is mystery.

Hallowe'en was once part of that mystery. Now it has become an excuse for violence, for the often ugly acting-out of frustration and aggression. It is another horrendous false expectation—that we should be encouraged to act out everything we feel. On my route from New York to northwest Connecticut there are, at the Hallowe'en season, effigies of dead people hanging from trees. On the streets of New York there are kids dressed like skeletons, ghosts, witches. There's no longer anything loving or affirmative about this holy day. What has the computer done in translating and retranslating All Hallow's Eve?

In the violence that is now part of Hallowe'en there is not only a threat of death, there is a terror of death. The streets are even less safe than they are at other times. In my apartment building there are a lot of kids. Their parents are unwilling to allow them to go out on the streets trick-or-treating. They go to the other apartments in our building, where the tenants are given little pumpkins to stick on our doors if we're willing to welcome the children with treats. But even this harmless trick-or-treating is a far cry from the original story of Hallowe'en. A symptom of what has happened is that in the world of copyediting the word *Hallowe'en* is now spelled *Halloween*, thereby desacralizing it even further. In a recent manuscript of mine I was saddened to learn that this spelling is now "correct." But when I talk about this holy day, I am talking about Hallowe'en.

For Christians, Hallowe'en is fulfilled in the gift of the birth of Jesus far more than in the death of Jesus. What a magnificent mystery of the Word Made Flesh! Christ, the power that created the universe, relinquished all power to come to us as one of us, mortal, human, walking the short road from the womb to the tomb. Often we stumble along, not knowing where we're going, but understanding that the journey is worth it because Jesus took it for us, shared it with us. Because the immortal God became mortal, we all share in the immortality as well as the mortality. And how can we begin to understand our immortality until we accept our mortality?

What I believe is so magnificent, so glorious, that it is beyond finite comprehension. To believe that the universe was created by a purposeful, benign Creator is one thing. To believe that this Creator took on human vesture, accepted death and mortality, was tempted, betrayed, broken, and all for love of us, defies reason. It is so wild that it terrifies some Christians who try to dogmatize their fear by lashing out at other Christians, because a tidy Christianity with all answers given is easier than one which reaches out to the wild wonder of God's love, a love we don't even have to earn.

In the Middle Ages when Hallowe'en was a feast of love and praise and hope, people talked of *the Mysterium Tremendum et Fascinans*: "The tremendous and fascinating mystery." The translation doesn't do the original justice, but when we forget the mystery and try to understand the Incarnation in terms of provable fact, our belief becomes a sounding brass and a clanging cymbal. It may be very loud indeed, but it is no longer a wondrous mystery, and it brings no joy. What has our translating computer done? The Mysterium Tremendum et Fascinans has come out as "God will get you if you don't watch out."

We've taken the words of the love of Christ back and forth into the computer until we've come to believe that the meat is tough—too tough for us to digest.

So the love of God has been turned upside down into the anger of God. If we believe that God is angry with us, no wonder kids put on ugly red and black Satan costumes, because anger is consistent with Satan and not with God. And if we believe that God is angry with us, how can Hallowe'en be anything other than a threat? And if we believe that God is angry with us, how can we believe in the Incarnation? The Incarnation was *the* manifestation of God's love, not a display of bad temper.

Janis Ian sings a song about all the ills on earth, and about the distress the angels feel over what is going on. The angels ask, "What about the love?" Where is it? What went wrong?

Just a few days ago I read in a reputable church magazine that by the year two thousand the mainline churches will be dead. I don't believe it. Not unless we keep on feeding expressions of our faith into the translator, hoping they'll come up with something easier to believe.

If it's easy to believe, it's not worth believing. If it's easy to believe it doesn't offer any real challenge, and perhaps that's why some TV evangelists and other well-known religious figures have indulged in behavior that seems contrary to their expressed beliefs. If it's easy to believe, it's no guide to behaviour.

A friend gave me a clipping from a North Carolina paper in which the Baptist leaders have determined that forty-six percent of the population is already damned to hell.

What about the love? What about the love?

In the same issue of the paper was an article about the cross being the "in thing" to wear this season if you want to be in fashion. Understanding what the cross is about has nothing to do with it; it has become a fashion statement. One young ordained woman said that when she wears her clerical collar on the street she often gets rude and ugly comments, but she wasn't prepared to have another woman rush up to her asking, "Where did you get that outfit?"

What about the love? What about the love?

Last winter when I was intelligent enough to accept a speaking engagement in Honolulu in February, a Lutheran woman asked me, "Why are the mainline denominations shrinking in numbers, and why are the sects and fundamentalists growing?"

The sects and fundamentalists are growing because they offer black-and-white answers to all the unanswerable questions. The frightened person is given all the rules and assured that the few people who keep the rules and accept the answers to the unanswerable questions will be saved, and everybody else will be damned. The damnation of others seems to be a large part of the pleasure of accepting the answers to the unanswerable questions. X and Y cannot be saved unless Z is in hell.

We live in a frightening world where there are wars which appear to be uncontrollable. Random acts of violence increase. Wife abuse, child abuse, racial abuse—human abuse—are all around us. No wonder some people run in fear to the enclosures which promise safety. (Were the Branch Davidians safe? Are the Muslim fundamentalist terrorists safe?) No wonder some people cling to the laws which give the answers but no laughter, no joy. And no love. What about the love?

Where is the laughter? Where is the joy? Why are we losing numbers? Are we? In my church we do not, thank God, give all the answers. But are we still too reasonable? Have we forgotten the Mysterium Tremendum et Fascinans? Have we forgotten the compassion and love of Christ in favor of being politically correct?

In one of Dick Francis's novels his protagonist tells a story of the man set upon by thieves. He is lying in the gutter, bleeding, half dead, and the priest passes by, hurrying on his way to Jerusalem to preach his famous sermon on compassion. The Levite passes by, too afraid of breaking one of the laws to stop and help. Then two sociologists come by, and they do stop, and they look down on the poor, bleeding man. And one sociologist says to the other, "Whoever did this needs help from us."

What about the love? What about the love?

Do we make demands on ourselves that are so unreasonable they are unworkable? Are our expectations radically false? Roger Williams came to this country seeking freedom of religion and became pastor of a church in Massachusetts. After a while he decided that out of all the churches in his town, only the people in his own church were worthy of salvation, and he announced this very loudly. Rather predictably, this announcement was not taken kindly by the other churches, and he was asked to leave. So he took his congregation and moved to what is now Providence, Rhode Island. After a while he decided that of all the people in his congregation, only he and his wife were worthy of salvation. And then he began to have doubts about his wife.

And then—and then Roger Williams understood that nobody, nobody is worthy enough to be saved. Salvation is a matter of grace. Yea! Alleluia! No matter how many merit badges we accumulate, they are not enough. That is the point of the parable of the workers in the vineyard. We don't get paid for good works, we get loved!

What about the love? What about the love?

That's what! It's the Mysterium Tremendum et Fascinans. It's the energy of Christ informing mortal matter. It's the believing that permeates our being.

If we are infused, enthused with this joy and this wonder, then it will be infectious, far more infectious than answers to unanswerable questions. God loves us! We are not worthy—God save us from the worthy. We are saved by grace and bathed with love, and if we remember that with sheer, hilarious joy, then our numbers will stop dwindling (and numbers are something else we should stop worrying about).

Remember: Our Lord said feed my sheep, not count them.

Grace is what it's all about, Lord of Lords in human vesture, Christ come to us as the mortal Jesus.

Let us remember that grace as we contemplate All Hallow's Eve. There are some Christians who refuse to allow their children to have anything to do with Hallowe'en because it is seen to be Satanic and unchristian. No apple bobbing, no pumpkins with lighted candles, no pumpkin pie. When my kids were little Hallowe'en was gentler than it is now, but isn't it foolish to throw out a holy day because the original meaning has been distorted? Shouldn't we try to recover the story and its central truth, rather than to wipe it out?

On Hallowe'en I will especially remember my parents. I will especially remember my husband, and I will remember him going down a dark road with our children so they wouldn't be frightened as they went to the neighbors with their Unicef boxes and their little paper bags which would soon be filled with homemade cookies and apples, and we didn't have to worry about wicked people putting razor blades in apples or poison into brownies. I will remember my husband borrowing an old raccoon coat for his costume and pretending to be a bear, and our children felt safe and protected with him.

I will remember a little cousin who was drowned when he was two, and a beloved older cousin who was a mentor to me and lived into her nineties. And I will believe on All Hallow's Eve as I believe every day that they still *are,* going from strength to strength in God's love.

Let's play back that translating computer which has mistranslated so much throughout the centuries that we're forgetting the original story, the story that has to do with God's inestimable love. Jesus' life illustrated for us the wonder that matter matters, every tiny atom of each one of us, and of all creation. Let's put into the translator "the spirit is willing but the flesh is weak," and maybe it will come out, "the spirit is singing and the flesh is part of the tremendous and fascinating mystery."

God says, "I love you! I love you enough to come and be with you. And because I live forever, you will, too."

All Hallow's Eve: one of the holiest of our holy days. Let our expectations of it be of love, the original love that informs all our holy days.

We have false expectations of our holy days, of our churches, of each other. We have false expectations of our friends. Jesus did not. He had expectations, but they were not false, and when they were not met, he did not fall apart. He was never taken in by golden calves!

Friendship not only takes time, it takes a willingness to drop false expectations, of ourselves, of each other. Friends—or lovers—are not always available to each other. Inner turmoils can cause us to be unhearing when someone needs us, to need to receive understanding when we should be giving understanding. We are not static in any relation. The world we live in is unstable under our feet, and so we grab at any security we can. We all want security. I do. I want to go to bed knowing that my family is all right; that the world is a safe enough place so that I can go to sleep knowing that the night will be at least moderately quiet (that's the best we can hope for in a big city), and that I'll be allowed to wake up in the morning and get on with the business of the day. I want to know that my friends will always be available for me when I need them—and vice versa. We make golden calves out of false expectations and are horrified when they turn out to be metal or clay, not flesh and blood at all.

The more I am aware of the danger of idols, the more I am able to enjoy fully the iconic pleasures I do have, pleasures of family and friends and sunsets and good music and my nearly new kitchen stove and all the little things we are given to rejoice in. I love the small group of women with whom I meet weekly to discuss whatever book we have chosen and what it means in our lives and in our understanding of Christ. We do not try to coerce each other, even when we disagree. We try to listen to each other, and to God. Therefore, this group is for me another icon, and one that helps me to keep my eyes and ears open, and my mind ready to move and grow in understanding.

I love cooking dinner for my friend Barbara, who now shares my apartment. It is a pleasure to have food and drink ready for her when she comes in late from a heavy day at work in the Presiding Bishop's office. I love cooking for a table full of friends or for so many people that we have to serve the meal buffet style, because eating together is iconic for me, and it is a special joy to have the privilege of preparing the food. Creamed spinach can be an icon!

There have been times in my life when I have made unreasonable demands, when I have, in fact, allowed an icon to turn into an idol. As an adolescent I had crushes on some of my teachers, on a few writers, and on a few actors, for I was a young woman in the 1930s and '40s, in a day when there were great theatrical stars. Today, in the world of theatre, television, movies, we have celebrities—successes. I am grateful that I worked in the theatre when there were stars, true stars; when talent was respected— genius, rather than personality. Success is thin unless it is supported by the firm ground of commitment to excellence, to the drudgery of long rehearsals, to being willing to learn and grow in the difficult art of giving audiences a transcendental experience, something that is beyond teaching, or amusement, but is, indeed, an icon.

Nowadays in order to be a success you have to have notoriety, any kind of notoriety. A young woman skater tries to cripple a rival. An athlete is accused of murdering his ex-wife and her friend, and is a star on the news and in the papers. These people are heroes? I want to be able to respect my heroes, to believe them to be honourable, courageous, decent. Notoriety is not usually an attribute of heroes. I fear for those who admire notoriety and therefore are willing to emulate wickedness. If this fear is naive, it is naive.

I remember a cold November evening, the first autumn after I had graduated from college, when I stood with one of my roommates at the stage door entrance to a Broadway theatre. We had just seen a fine performance by Eva LeGallienne, and we wanted to see her come out of the stage door. We didn't plan to speak to her. We just

PENTICTON UNITED CHURCH
LIBRARY

wanted to see this great actress leave the theatre and to pay her silent homage.

We had been standing there, in the shadows, waiting, for at least half an hour when the stage doorman came ambling out, peered around, and saw us. We tried to melt back into the shadows but he asked us, kindly, what we were doing.

When we told him we were waiting to catch a glimpse of Miss LeGallienne he said, "She left early tonight, hon. Everybody's gone home. Do you want to come in and see her dressing room? I'll show you."

Awed, dazzled, we followed him, up the steps, down a long hall. He took a key off a rack of labeled keys and led us to the nearest door and opened it. The room had a faint odor of make-up and Chypre perfume. On a stand on the long shelf of the make-up table was the wig Miss LeGallienne wore for the play. The kindly doorman picked up a linen towel that covered a tray, and there, tidily laid out, was her make-up: brushes, little pots of rouge, a small Sterno for heating her mascara.

And that dressing table was, for me, an icon of all that is good and hard-working and honourable in the theatre.

"She's a good lady," the doorman said, scratching his white hair. "You actresses?"

My roommate said, "Yes. At least I want to be."

He looked at me, smiling.

"She's the real actress," I said. "I just write." I kept looking at the make-up table. It was clean and professional. There was nothing extraneous. At the far end was a vase of autumn leaves and chrysanthemums. Costumes were neatly hung on a rack.

For two stage-struck girls the old doorman was an angel, and the entire dressing room was an icon of theatre, theatre that existed to open the minds and hearts of the audience. Today the ideal of theatre is most closely met in the regional theatres, but back at the beginning of the 1940s Broadway was still the Great White Way. A play had to make enough money to keep open, but more important than the money was the offering of the vision of the great playwrights to a hungry audience. We wanted to honour the leading men and women who were stars, not celebrities—people who cared passionately about their art rather than self-aggrandizement. Eva Le-Gallienne had a vision of bringing great plays in repertory to ordinary people at ordinary prices. We admired her. And we came close to idolizing her.

There's the rub; an icon can far too easily become an idol. Idols always bring disaster to the idolater. An icon is an open door to the Creator; when it becomes an idol, the door slams in your face.

Later I had the privilege of working in two Broadway plays with this great actress, and I learned to understand her as a complex human being who taught me a great deal about art and life and vulnerability and reality. That glimpse of her dressing room was iconic. I learned to see her as an icon, too, as I watched her continuing struggle to become a better actress, a more complete person. When I thought about her most creatively, most truly, she was an icon for me. When I wanted her to be more than she was, the icon became idol.

Now this great actress is dead, having lived into her nineties. Recently a friend of hers sent me a small book of daily prayers from Miss LeG's (as we called her) bedside. Many passages have been marked, and this little book is signed with her unique signature and is, for me, an icon of fidelity to art, a fidelity which was her response to God's calling.

I'm grateful that our friendship grew to a quiet place where I could let her be who she was, a great actress, but fully human. False expectations can cause great damage, particularly among Christians.

A woman in my church, Rachel, lost her twenty-three-year-old daughter in a tragic accident; she lost her legs and then took several weeks to die. Rachel said, "I can't pray. People think I'm terrible because I can't pray."

—Lay off her! I thought of those who would criticize. Insisting that people be able to pray at all times is one of our false expectations of each other, as human beings, as Christians.

"That's all right," I assured her. "We're praying for you. You don't need to do it yourself." She looked at me hopefully, and I continued, "There have been times in my life, too, when I have been unable to pray, but other people have prayed for me. That's what being part of the body of Christ is about."

"I'm angry at God!" she said. "People think I'm terrible because I'm angry at God."

Again I tried to reassure her. "It's all right to be angry at God. I'll bet God is angry at what happened to your child, too."

"But people say we should never be angry at God . . ."

"They haven't read the psalms, then. The psalmists got furious at God and never hesitated to say so. God loves us as we are, in our pain and anger as much as in our easy times." Why are Christians always supposed to repress pain, anguish, doubt, to be cheery, faithful, happy people all the time? That is not what the Good News is all about. Jesus was not happy all the time. When his cousin, John, was beheaded, he grieved. When his disciples all abandoned him in the garden he was anguished. He met hardness of heart with a flare of anger. The human part of Jesus was totally human. For our sakes he even expressed doubt in the garden and on the cross. Why do we expect more of ourselves than we do of God Incarnate?

The media feed on our false expectations, first, of ourselves, then of families, friends, lovers—false expectations of life, of success. We worship at the altar of worldly success, but we have no idea what real success is. It is not acclaim, wealth, beauty, unless these are inner and not outer qualities.

After the Resurrection Jesus was recognized not by his outer qualities—he was never recognized by sight—but by his inner qualities, his Christ-self.

In Antarctica my idea of success was making it in and out of the zodiacs each day! And relaxing enough so that I could enjoy the beauty of the icebergs, the deep, dark water turbulent with breaking ice, the strange, cold skies. They were a potent icon of God's creation.

At bedtime in my cabin I read Evening Prayer and Scripture, and looked at my tiny icon of the Trinity. I don't really need a picture of either an angel or a penguin to remind me of their iconic quality. Yes, intimacy is dangerous, but we are not human without it.

Do angels know intimacy? I am not sure. We are not told. I suspect they know an intimacy far beyond our human capacity. During my life there have been people who have been God-bearers and, therefore, icons for me. But, alas, I have also been tempted to put too much on these people, as I did when I first knew Miss LeG, and so I've turned them into idols, and that is disastrous. I have expected them to solve my problems, to give me answers, to take the place of God in my life. When I was a young woman during the Second World War there was a French pianist, a refugee, who represented to me the wonder of music, the structure of the fugue, the anguish of discord which leads to the resolution of harmony. He was a little older than I, better read, handsome, desirable. And I put too much on him, expected too much of him.

When he let me down, betrayed me, I was devastated. But ultimately it was the best thing he could have done for me. He toppled off the pedestal I had put him on, and the marble statue broke into fragments. I saw the man I had imprisoned in stone to be vulnerable, vain, gifted, but totally human. When I was able to accept him as he was, we became good friends and remained so until his death. This was an enormous blessing in my life, but it couldn't happen until all traces of the idol had been taken away.

I have gone through this process with three people who have been major influences in my life. One was someone I thought was totally holy, and who did indeed embody great holiness. But there was also a shadow that was not acknowledged and that had become septic—and that infected wound was played out in unacceptable and terrible ways, not only unworthy of my friend, but in violent contradiction to the holiness. In the end I was able to accept the shadow *without losing sight of* the holiness, and our friendship was deepened.

Often when I teach a writer's workshop I am asked, "What do you do, in your journal-type books, when you are writing sensitive things about real people?"

My reply is, "When I am writing about something that might invade privacy or hurt someone, I translate. I invent another situation which has the same emotional or spiritual impact."

So that is what I have just done. What I have written about Miss LeGallienne is true to my memory of this great artist. But I have also "made up" some idols who are not, in reality, the people I have idolized. The reality I want to talk about is the idolization, which is always tragic. When it happens, I have to remember the warnings of the psalmist and hope that by grace the idol will be turned back into icon. I wonder if I have finally learned. A mortal is a more dangerous idol than a golden calf.

Talking about golden calves is another way of talking about idols. We don't have to collect all our necklaces and earrings and melt them down and give them to Aaron to make a golden calf. Anything we love to the exclusion of the Maker of us all is a golden calf.

For me the penguin is my present icon for intimacy. It is amazingly difficult to turn a penguin into an idol.

At the bottom of the world I looked at the penguins, smiling at their ludicrousness as they waddled about, chattering, scolding, announcing. They are noisier on land than they are in the sea, because they are sea creatures, not land creatures. They stay on land only long enough to lay their eggs, incubate them, and nourish their fledglings until they are able to swim. Then they return to the sea, which is their true element.

I wonder about us, us human creatures, and where our true element is to be found. We cannot go back to the Garden of Eden, so perhaps we will not find it again until after our human deaths. If we had not left the garden too soon, before we had matured enough to be ready, we would know where home is, where our Maker wants us to be, and what we are supposed to do.

The penguins taught me by how much sheer fun they had during their time on land, and the even greater fun of flopping into the water as they went to find food for their chicks, swimming as they collected fish or krill, and then belly-flopping back onto the stony shore, padded by the thick feathers on their fronts.

Even if we have lost our way, we are still supposed to enjoy all the wonders God has given us, many of which we simply take for granted. When we enjoy something wholly, as the penguins enjoyed their play, we are not taking that enjoyment for granted. We are part of it, and in our lack of self-consciousness we too are part of the Mysterium Tremendum et Fascinans.

Relaxing in the penguins' delight added to my awe at the incredible, indescribable loveliness of the Antarctic Peninsula. The sheer splendor of this part of the planet that was still in the ice age was staggering. So was the afternoon when three humpback whales played about our little ship.

One of our lecturers was studying whale flukes, so he asked everybody to take as many snapshots as possible of the flukes. But the whales refused to fluke for us. They looked ready; cameras were cocked; and then the whales would drop down below the surface of the water. A few moments later they would spout, and cameras were readied again.

"They're teasing us!" someone said, and it seemed that they were. Then suddenly they dove down, waving their glorious flukes in a grand gesture of farewell, and disappeared.

As we sailed further and further south we went to bed by daylight, for the hours of darkness grew fewer and fewer, until we reached the Antarctic continent itself and moved into almost complete daylight. There were only a few hours of dark in the very earliest hours of the morning, when most of us were sound asleep in our bunks. I tried to get enough sleep so that I would have the strength to enjoy this fabulous and mysterious continent. This meant not having false expectations of myself, but missing a few evening documentary movies in order to get adequate rest. It meant accepting that I was not completely healed from the accident, but not letting my bodily ills themselves become idols. It was a balancing act in which I was not entirely successful—but successful enough so that the beauty always reached me. And it was a beauty so mysteriously radiant that it was impossible to turn it into an idol!

3

FAMILY VALUES

 My husband and I tried to teach our children values, and I suppose they were what today would be called "family values." We believed that ordinary courtesy was freeing rather than stifling. We believed that our own faith in God was the best way to show our children the love of God.

Lately we've heard a lot about family and family values, both pro and con, as both icon and idol, until we hardly know what they are anymore. I suspect that some of the public people who talk most loudly about family values don't have any. If Scripture is our source, we are assured that families are complex, to put it mildly, starting with the first family, Adam and Eve and their children, Cain, Abel, and Seth. It is a relief to know that not all families are that tragic, but there's little indication in Scripture that there were any "normal" or "functional" families, with mother, father, children, and no problems. Indeed, such a "functional family" is one of our twentieth-century idols.

For one thing, a family like that would offer us no stories. In any case, I don't think the "normal" or "functional" family exists. I've certainly never encountered one. *Functional* and *dysfunctional* have become pop words, and pop words are often our defense against the reality of what we are talking about. To label someone as dysfunctional is easier than to look at the person whose life is in such disarray that ordinary living becomes too much to face. Compassion hurts; labels are easier. Labels are, in fact, a kind of golden calf.

Find me a family in Scripture which is not dysfunctional! (And why do we spell it dysfunctional instead of disfunctional?)

Ants live in a completely functional society. A dysfunctional ant is wiped out. The people who lived on Camazotz, one of the planets in my book *A Wrinkle in Time*, lived in a completely functional society. Like the ants, if they did not conform to that society's norm, they were wiped out, eliminated.

Thank God scriptural families are different and much more like most of our human families. Noah's family laughed derisively at him for building an ark. Ishmael and Isaac quarreled, as did Jacob and Esau. Surely King David's family was anything but harmonious. Moses' family was certainly complex, but it was because of the love of his mother and sister that Moses survived infancy at a time when the Pharaoh ordered that all the male children of the Hebrews be killed. If Moses had not been put in the basket of bulrushes, what would have happened to one of the most famous of all our Bible stories?

But Moses was raised at Pharaoh's court, in great luxury. He was well educated, well fed, well clothed. I recently had a fascinating taxi ride during which the driver talked to me about Moses and shared his conviction that Moses had actually been Pharaoh for a while, but had left all the pomp and circumstance of the court to return to his people. I've never been able to find proof or disproof of this, but it is interesting that we know nothing of Moses between his discovery in the bulrushes and verse 11 of chapter 2 of Exodus, "And it came to pass in those days, when Moses was grown, that he went out unto his brethren, and looked on their burdens." There is the same kind of gap in our knowledge of Moses' life that there is in our knowledge of Jesus': after Jesus astounded the elders in the temple when he was twelve, we know nothing of him until he started his public ministry.

Moses led his people out of Egypt, across the Red Sea, and to within sight of the Promised Land, though he died before that land was entered. He gave his people the Law, and he talked with God, and the brilliance of God was on his face so that the people could not bear to look at him until he covered his face.

Despite the glory of God Moses had shown them, the people became restless. When Moses was too long up the mountain, conversing with the Lord, Aaron made a golden calf, an idol, and the people worshipped the idol. Oy veh!

"You are a stiff-necked people!" God cried in the 32nd chapter of Exodus, and this was something the Creator frequently had cause to say of us mortals. This time the Lord was so outraged at the golden calf which the people had made, and which they were worshipping, that he was ready to wipe them out, destroy them.

But Moses talked God out of his anger with the arguments, so familiar to us, "What will the Joneses think?" What, O Lord, will the Egyptians think of you, if you have brought your people out of Egypt, taken us safely across the Red Sea—what will they think of you if you destroy us now? What kind of a god will they think you are?

And God heard Moses and "relented from the harm which he said He would do to His people."

God more often wants to save us than to zotz us; we are God's people, and God's people of course includes all of us who are stiff-necked enough to turn away from truth and worship the twentieth-century equivalent of golden calves which are so tempting to our affluent society. Like Aaron, we rationalize and excuse what we are doing.

At the Solemn Profession service of an Episcopal nun, the preacher contrasted her vows of poverty, chastity, and obedience, with the world's money, sex, and power. We need to go back to those three ancient vows. We are all supposed to be poor in spirit. We are all supposed to be chaste, and for most of us chastity does not mean sexlessness, but sex that is expressed in love, not power. We are all supposed to be obedient to that love, but we forget love whenever we want power over someone else. We human beings mess it up, over and over again, but God comes into our lives to help us overcome our stiff-neckedness. Indeed, God so loved the world that he sent his only-begotten Son to live with us and teach us how to be the fully human creatures our Maker has always planned for us to be.

How often the image of the good shepherd is used throughout Scripture! The good shepherd goes out into the wilderness after the one lost sheep and brings it home, rejoicing. There does seem to be more excitement over the return of the lost sheep than there is over all the good little sheep who stayed home. "There is joy in the presence of the angels of God over one sinner who repents."

That may seem a little unfair to all the good people who have never done any wrong and have nothing to repent about, but since I am not one of them (and neither is anybody else I am close to) it really isn't much of a problem. I never get through a day without needing to repent over something, and I think that's true of most of us. Mostly what we repent of isn't enormous—we don't push drugs, we don't murder, we don't commit adultery. What I need to ask forgiveness for is usually lack of sensitivity to another's need because I am too tired or too busy to hear. Or I lose my temper without adequate cause and say sharp and hurtful words. Or I fall for the lure of the media and think that life should be fair and growl when it isn't.

And then, when we're hit by the ordinary troubles that come to most lives, we feel, "Why me? Why did this happen to me? It's not fair. Life is not supposed to be like this."

But it *is* like this, often grossly unfair, often tragic, and when life disappoints us and our illusions vanish, we too often turn to worship our twentieth-century equivalents of golden calves.

A few weeks ago I read a book of Frederick Buechner's in which his illusion of being part of a perfect family was rudely shattered when he discovered that one of his daughters had *anorexia nervosa* and had nearly starved herself to death. The illusion of the perfect family is another of America's golden calves. Yet maybe the most important thing about family values is the acceptance of each other as the imperfect, complex creatures we are, but loved and loving nevertheless. Family is of the utmost importance to me. But my family is no more perfect than Buechner's, and I suspect that is the way of most families. We love, trust, get hurt, sometimes outraged, and we love and trust anyhow, because that's the best way to let our love grow.

Our tendency to turn from God and worship golden calves is exacerbated when our vision of God stops with the anthropomorphic, patriarchal God of Exodus. Moses had to talk God out of eradicating all his stiff-necked people who turned from him and roused his anger. This punitive God is far from the God, the Abba, Daddy, Papa, Jesus showed us, and if we do not make the transition from the angry to the loving God who does indeed note the fall of every sparrow and who counts the very hairs of our head, we have misunderstood the Gospel, the Good News of God's incredible love.

Refusing to accept God's love because we're unworthy—of course we're unworthy!—is another golden calf. Sometimes I think the people of Hebrew Scripture were more able to understand that God loved them in spite of their stiff-neckedness than we who have been given the Gospel. The God they talked to may have looked in their minds' eyes more like Moses than Moses himself, but they talked with God, shouted with God, argued with God, even expected God to change his mind if they shouted loudly enough. The psalms are full of joyous cries of praise and outraged bellowings of self-pity and anger. Will you forget us forever, O Lord? Why don't you turn your anger from us? Come back! Rise up like a giant refreshed with wine and turn and save us! There is no doubt that God was present in the lives of the Hebrew children, even when they got impatient with him (yes, him, for their God was certainly patriarchal) and built golden calves.

But what about us? We've become too polite. We don't laugh and cry with God. We've forgotten the excitement of the Good News. What greater sign of the extraordinary, lavish, marvelous love of God than the Incarnation! God so loved the world and all of us in it that God elself came to live with us as one of us! Is it so good that we're afraid to believe it?

The ancient Hebrews believed that if they were honestly sorry for whatever ill they had committed, God would turn from his anger and love them again. They truly did believe in the Good Shepherd who is written about so beautifully in the 23rd psalm. It is interesting that the affirmation of the 23rd psalm comes immediately after the cry of anguish in the 22nd, "My God, my God, why have you forsaken me?" Is it really so difficult to believe that when we falter and stray and get lost God will come after us and carry us home?

I learned recently that a certain rabbi felt that the image (icon) of the Lord as shepherd was an insult to the Most High, because the shepherd was at the bottom of the societal rung, was a nobody. But that's all right! Even in Hebrew Scriptures God makes All Power into nothing. God is the great potentate who abandons majesty in order to show tender love to sheep like us. As for sheep, it is well known that the sheep is the stupidest of all animals.

I believe that when I do wrong, God is hurt, as I am hurt when someone I love does something wrong or unworthy. I'm not sure about anger. Jesus did get angry on occasion, but he never stayed stuck in anger. Instead, he felt the pain of compassion, of understanding, of wanting the best from people and often getting the worst. And he told us that all our heavenly Father wanted was for us to say, "I'm sorry, Daddy. I want to come home," and God would promptly give a big party, rejoicing that the strayed lamb had returned.

Those who do not believe in a loving God do not enjoy parties!

When my children were little I wanted to have every evening meal be a party. We always ate by candlelight, and if my breakfasts and school lunches left something to be desired, I tried to make the evening meal a special one, taking turns with the children's favourite dishes. My icon of what I wanted my family to be is the dinner table, all of us disparate people sitting around it together, holding hands to say grace before eating, thanking God for food and shelter and love, while being aware of the terrible needs around us and asking God to help us to help in whatever way we can.

I love Crosswicks, the old house in the country where Hugh and I raised our children, where so much of our married life was built. Crosswicks is, I hope, an icon for me, an icon of family and all that is best in family life despite our failures with each other, our stupid quarrels, our blind lacks in love. It is still an icon even though it now belongs to my son and daughter-in-law and not to me. After my husband died there was no way I could have kept it up, single-handed. I am grateful indeed that it is still in the family, that I can come for occasional vacations, for Christmas. But it is not mine any-more, and that is right and proper. And it is still an icon. If it has to be *mine* it is an idol.

I do not believe that there has been a really innocent time since Adam and Eve left the Garden, but the world was perhaps more innocent when my children were little than it is now, despite the fact that the planet was still a warring place, that we were terrified of nuclear warfare with Russia, that we had an ambiguous war with Korea and were heading into an even more ambiguous one in Viet Nam, that we were surrounded by the suspicion and fear exempli-fied by such people as Senator Joseph McCarthy.

In our little dairy farm village in New England nobody was very rich and nobody was very poor—that distinction was to come later. People went to church, even if they didn't think very much about the God they were called to worship.

Nevertheless, when we moved on February first of 1960 from our rural dairy farm village to the wilds of the island of Manhattan, the city was still moderately safe. Drugs had not yet become a prob-lem. There were no protective metal blinds or grills over shop win-dows or doors; the proprietor shut and locked the door to the shop and that was all the precaution needed. The proliferation of porno-graphic bookstores and movies was still over the horizon. The di-vorce rate had not yet passed the fifty percent mark.

Things have changed. The gap between the very rich and the very poor grows wider. Families, including mine, are scattered. Mis-understanding is prevalent, among nations, peoples, families. And yet, and yet—family is still an icon for me. For seven years I lived with my granddaughters as they moved through their college years, taking time out to work and earn money for their education. Char-lotte was with me steadily, Lena in and out. Now the time has come when they have moved into their own apartments, only a few blocks away, but still into their own places, into the fullness of their own lives. I miss them, but I know that it is right and proper, just as it is right and proper that Crosswicks now belongs to my son and daughter-in-law. And my granddaughters and I continue to be close together, go to the movies, out to a special dinner, or have an evening at home in my apartment, cooking dinner and then watching a movie. But it is different. Some icons have their own time spans, and we must learn that part of their wondrousness includes letting go.

A goodly number of people expected me to fall apart when my granddaughters moved out, but while I have treasured my time with these two wonderful young women, I am also treasuring my time alone, playing the piano again on a regular basis. While my husband was alive I had my special piano time between six and seven in the evening, before I cooked dinner. But living with a husband and living with granddaughters are two quite different things, and somehow or other piano practise time went down the drain. I am enjoying going back to it, working on my memorized sonatas, fugues, and other treasured pieces. I am enjoying a few quiet evenings alone, and it is good to go to bed without one ear open for one or other of these two young women, out late with friends. I am enjoying not stepping over running shoes and tea cups. I am enjoying being down to one dog and one cat. I am starting an entirely new journey, and this is always a challenge. I have a new apartment mate, a friend I have known for over a decade, and we are rediscovering each other in a new and delightful way. Endings are beginnings!

And what about my childhood family? I've written about my husband and our children, my family as a grown-up, my life with my granddaughters, but what about my family when I was a child?

I read recently that in times of trouble we are supposed to look back on all the happy memories of our childhoods. I've written a good bit about my early years, mostly about insensitive and punitive teachers who taught me only that they considered me stupid and unattractive. But surely there are other memories?

Of course there are. But as I looked back I found no happy ones. There were many that were not unhappy. There were even occasional joys, such as my first glimpse of the stars at my grandmother's house on the beach in north Florida. But the happy memories—and I have been blessed with many—do not start until my high school years. The good memories of childhood—good, not happy—are mostly sensory: being given my first taste of ice-cold ginger ale on a hot city summer night; coming back to the city after a few weeks in the country, going to bed, and hearing all the familiar city sounds: the Lexington Avenue trolley car, the Third Avenue El, taxi horns, bus brakes, sirens, shouts, all the city noises which were the sounds of my city, and falling asleep with their strange lullaby in my ears; hearing the bells of the horse-drawn knife sharpeners' or pot menders' carts. Then there was the loveliness of the lighted trees all up and down Park Avenue at Christmastime; the mystery of the Egyptian wing at the Metropolitan Museum; the snow transforming the city streets into beauty, at least for the first few hours.

Perhaps the closest to real happiness was opening a storybook sent me from England by my grandfather. English printer's ink in those days had a very different smell from American printer's ink, and I would open the book and press my nose against the pages and sniff the delectable odor of English ink which meant, for me, that I would soon have the pleasure of reading a good story.

But because I was a child and my parents were too preoccupied with their own, very real problems to realize the strange, psychic abuse to which I was being subjected, I accepted my classmates' and teachers' assessment of me as the worthless one.

We all want to belong, child or adult. It is a basic human need. I didn't belong.

My memories of my parents become more complete after we left New York when I was twelve, and we wandered through the Alps trying to find a place where my father, with his mustard-gassed lungs, could breathe. I remember the times when, for no reason except that it seemed necessary, we would go to a good hotel or restaurant for a festive meal, often marred by an argument over the expense. But it is only recently that I remembered the end of our first summer abroad, when one day my parents and I got into a car and I was told that they had decided that I was to go to boarding school. We drove to the school, I was taken in to meet the matron, my parents said good-bye to me, and they left.

I had had no warning. It all happened in a few hours.

The matron fitted me with the school uniform and told me that if I thought boarding school was going to be like the stories by Angela Brazil, a popular writer of boarding school stories, I had another thing coming. She was right.

My parents, I learned later, had once again used me as a battle ground. My mother wanted me to go to the local French village school. My father did not think I would get an adequate education there, and thought I would learn to speak French with the local accent. He won the argument, and I don't think my parents realized how abrupt this transition was for me, or how difficult. School had already been in session for a week; groups had been formed; I was totally an outsider. The first few weeks were sheer hell and, except for the beauty of the countryside, the views of Lake Geneva, and across the lake to the French Alps, the rest was not much better. I'm glad this memory did not surface earlier, for only now am I old enough to understand my parents' own problems at the time. I'm not sure how much I would have learned in the village school; I didn't learn anything during the two years in that boarding school except how to survive. Barely.

I remember the vacations, when I would come "home" from boarding school. The first year I was in exile, so were my parents, in a small villa in Chamonix, under the shadow of Mont Blanc, where the mountain hid the sun so that there were only a few hours of daylight in December and the cold was unremitting. Every night the ink froze—those were the days when we still filled our pens with ink from bottles! Chamonix, which had been a famous tourist town, was nearly empty because of the Depression. There was almost no fresh food, and the village was hurting from lack of tourists. The unemployed mountain guides went hunting and brought home rabbits for us to cook.

The big hotel which overlooked our tiny villa opened for two weeks at Christmastime, and when I arrived for my vacation, my father had bought the English Christmas magazines with their beautiful pictures, and we would put on skis and schüss into the village for a pre-prandial drink; in those days I could drink hot chocolate loaded with whipped cream and never worry about calories. It was cold, cold in Chamonix and there was something unreal about the brief flare of festive activity. I remember the ice-skating in the late afternoon when the stars were already shining in a black sky. At the side of the skating rink were white-napped tables loaded with hot drinks and all kinds of sweet cakes to allure the tourists. I remember one man in a black beret who skated alone, his hands behind his back, doing slow figure eights.

For me, the main thing was the escape from boarding school, and I tried not to dwell on the fact that I would have to return. I also began to realize my parents' unhappiness, their alienation from the city where their friends had been artists and their lives had been full of music and theatre and books and art. I was not unhappy during that vacation; neither was I happy. The playground for the rich that was nearly dead because of the Depression was a metaphor for my own feelings.

My mother was oppressed by the great mountain which over-shadowed the village, by the snow which was so steady and so deep that no attempt was made to clear it. Great rollers pressed down certain streets and paths to level them for traffic. It was nearly as white a world as Antarctica, but whereas Antarctica showed no trace of human beings and all our various artifacts, Chamonix in the midst of all the snow proclaimed, first, the lack of people other than the villagers, and, during the two weeks the Grand Hotel was open, the tourists who were counted on to bring in enough revenue for the villagers to survive the winter. Like the penguins, the villagers were communal, but we were very aware that we needed each other, though my awareness was filtered through what my parents told me and through what I saw and heard as I put on my skis and did errands in the village. We did not leave the house without our skis, which were simply kept in the vestibule, ready for use. At that time of a total lack of what we now call affluence, there was only one kind of ski, on which one went marketing, skied cross country, or raced downhill.

The winter was cold and white and desolate, and I began to grow up. Perhaps what "grew me up" most was one afternoon when I came into the house, leaned my skis in the vestibule, and went up-stairs, looking for my mother. I could hear my father's typewriter clattering away downstairs in his frigid little study. My parents' bed-room door was pulled to, though not closed, and I pushed it open.

And there was my mother, stretched out in an abandon of anguish on the bed. I quickly backed out, and she never knew that I had seen her. For the first time I saw my parents as totally separated from me, caught in the pain of their own life. Somehow they had always been Mother and Father and so somehow were above all of the problems I recognized in myself and in most other people. I had a vague inkling of the trauma caused by the crash, the Depression, my father's gassed lungs, which had uprooted us from New York and sent us to the Alps, but I had not guessed at what all this had done to my parents. Seeing my mother lying abandoned to her grief awakened me.

So my mother, lying on her bed, not knowing that I had seen her, is for me an icon of the end of childhood. I was then and always have been a slow developer, but some of the transitions have come on me like thunder and lightning, and this was one of them. I did not record it in my journal. It was too private, too intense. Not all of our revelations are recorded, except in our hearts. Ultimately, as usually happens, the scene found words in a novel I wrote many years later.

Our memories which are essential to our wholeness can far too easily be turned from icon to idol. The good memories become idealized (idolized) until they bear little relation to reality. The bad memories, when they are carefully wrapped in pink cotton to keep them safe so they can be brought out and fondled, can be even more dangerous than the good ones.

It has been a great help to me that when I have written out an event and thereby objectified it, at least a little, I can usually let it go. For me it works best in story, though the first step is usually a journal entry. When I was grown up my mother would apologize to me for my odd childhood, and I would protest, "But Mother, look at all the material it's given me for my stories!" I wouldn't want to have missed a minute of it, though there's a lot of it I wouldn't want to have to live over. But we were a family, Mother, Father (for that's what I called them), and I, and I am grateful for their courage, their endurance, their integrity.

The Trinity is the icon of human family, and the wholeness and holiness of the Trinity is a mystery, so we should not be surprised that the family is a mystery, too.

4

BODIES

In Antarctica we stood looking and laughing at the penguins. They seemed to be completely at home in their bodies, rejoicing in what God had given them. Even when they were waddling on the land, they had a sense of rightness, that the way they were was as good as good could be. And when they were in the water they were as radiant and beautiful as angels!

What marvelous icons our human bodies should be! In Genesis we are told that we are made in the very image of God—yet, from the very beginning, we have dishonoured that image. Scripture reminds us most firmly that our bodies are temples of the Holy Spirit, and we must treat them with the love and respect they deserve.

Body and spirit are inseparable, and if we honour one, we honour the other. How is it that we have lost our spontaneity? It happened almost immediately, when Adam and Eve looked at their bodies and were ashamed. How can we be ashamed of what God has so lovingly made? Shame is an acquired characteristic, so I suppose it was cleverly suggested to them by the serpent. Children do not feel ashamed of their bodies unless someone plants the seed of shame. What susceptible creatures we are!

One of my very early memories which pleases me is an honouring of my body. It is a memory of being in my crib, up on my haunches, rocking back and forth and making a noise which was somewhere between a grunt and a hum and which indicated sheer physical contentment. Is that a happy memory? I'm not sure. It is one in which I was, even if unconsciously, affirming the goodness of my created body. What God has made is good. God made me, and at that moment in my crib I knew myself to be good.

The converse of this memory came a few years later when I was seven or eight. It is a single, brief memory of being in a swimming pool with quite a few other children, and some grown-ups, life guards, standing around. My parents and I must have been visiting friends in the country. I have only the memory of the pool, perhaps a pool at a country club. I was paddling around, not belonging to any group. I saw a small boy, about my own age, in a black wool tank suit. In the middle of the back was a round hole, about the size of a quarter, a perfect circle. As I swam by him, someone saw me as I reached out my finger and touched the skin within the circle.

What had I done that was wrong? All I remember was being made to feel that I had done a terrible thing, committed some fearful breach of etiquette. That white skin in the round hole in the black bathing suit was eminently touchable. We were children, nowhere near adolescence. I did not know why I was made to feel ashamed. I have no memory of before or after the incident, just a sense that I was made to feel guilty for something quite natural. I suppose this was at a time in human history when many people were still caught up in the heresy that spirit is good and flesh is evil. Other than that, I have no explanation.

I do know that my gentle touch of the small white round hole in the black bathing suit should have been an occasion of delight, of laughter, of affirmation of the goodness of creation, and of each one of us, bearing the precious, inestimable treasure of God's image.

My parents delighted in my child's body, but my schoolmates and teachers did not. I was laughed at, put aside as being imperfect, because one of my legs is longer than the other (most people have this problem to a small extent), and I had a bad knee which made me a slow and clumsy runner.

For some reason, still unknown, when I was three my right knee filled with fluid, felt hot and feverish, and my mother took me to a specialist who fitted me with a great leather and metal brace. I still remember it and how much I hated it. My mother confessed to me later that it made me cry, and it made her cry, too, so she took it off me and we never went back to that doctor. I suspect that was the wisest thing she could have done. But my schoolmates and teachers still found me clumsy in body, mind, and spirit, and made me see myself that way.

When I was barely old enough, my parents sent me to summer camp because they wanted to get me out of the heat of New York. I took with me the image of myself I had been given at school, and although later the camp became a happy place for me, for the first few summers it was clear to me that I was inadequate, that I did not fit in. I was clumsy and slow on the playing field, and that was how I was viewed everywhere, clumsy and slow.

One summer at camp when I was perhaps nine or ten years old, a group of girls invited me to join their secret society. I was thrilled. Little girls love clubs, and the secret ones are the most exciting. At last I was being asked to belong!

Of course there had to be an initiation. Most of it was pretty harmless, even being "inoculated" with a thorn, and then having toothpaste rubbed over the bead of blood to "sterilize" it.

But the final test of the initiation was for me to lick what were then called "the privates" of the other girls.

I wouldn't do it. I wanted to belong, but not at that price.

I didn't tell my parents. For many reasons I was a very private child.

Obviously the camp directors knew nothing of this club, and I suspect that it was short-lived. I continued to go to that camp for many summers, missing several when we were in Europe. By the time I was in high school and a senior camper, I had come to terms with who I was, and I had friends, and I loved the camp, the beauty of the mountains, the drive to the small lake where we swam, the occasional overnights when we rolled our army blankets into sleeping bags and slept out under the stars. Once a week we gathered together around the campfire, and beads were given out for—as I remember—good sportsmanship, trustworthiness, punctuality, courtesy, neatness, good citizenship—well, I think there were six or seven beads in all, and we wore them around our necks on shoelaces, treasuring them as though they were pearls. At the final campfire of the summer, pins were given out for girls who had especially merited them, and, most important of all, three cups, one for juniors, one for middlers, one for seniors. These cups were for the camper in each section who was the most all-around camper in all ways. I knew that I would never get a cup, much as I wanted one, because my lame leg kept me from being "all-around" as far as sports were concerned.

On the last campfire of my last summer as a camper (we seniors were to be junior counselors the next summer), I sat with the other girls from my tent, full of hope, because I expected to be given one of the pins. I had received one the previous summer, and surely I had thrown myself into all the activities even more fully this final summer. Beads were given out first, then certificates, then the pins, and finally the cups. When the last pin was given out my heart sank. I had not received a pin. I had not received a certificate. Nothing special. I could not understand it, and I tried very hard to control myself and not burst into tears. The junior cup was given out. The intermediate cup. Then I realized that there were two cups left. The senior cup was given to the girl on my left. Then the camp director held out the fourth, unexpected cup, and said that it was special, and for a special camper, who had shown her value in so many ways that the directors felt she ought to be recognized. Then she called on me.

That was a most wonderful moment. I was being honoured, all of me, bad knee, clumsiness, and all. It taught me a great deal, not only how to honour myself, but also how to honour others who might not, for one reason or other, fit the normal mold.

I believe that this specific honouring has helped me to honour the body all my life, my own body, the body of others. It has helped me to see wholeness. It has helped me to understand the fallacy of living in a culture where we elevate youth and bodily perfection to the exclusion of wisdom and the wonderful weatherings of a full life. It has helped me to understand the wholeness of the body and that every part of it is part of our wholeness and part of our sexuality.

Before I was married, one of my favorite cousins told me, "Sex is a third of a marriage, and it is a very important third, but it is only a third. There is also companionship, and quiet."

Companionship—the joining together of two people in conversation, in walking (Hugh and I used to love to walk around Washington Square in the late evening), in being with friends for shared meals, in going to the theatre or concerts, or in listening to records. There are many ways of companionship, and it is indeed a wonderful part of marriage.

Quiet. What did she mean by quiet? Those times when we are asleep together are obvious, but she meant more than that. Silent prayer time. Being time. Sitting together in church. (Oh, my God, I will never forget sitting by Hugh at a funeral, knowing that the cancer that was going to kill him was already in his body.) Times when suddenly and for no reason a deep quiet came upon us, and we were more totally together in that quiet than at any other time. I bless my beloved cousin for her advice.

The two times in my life with my husband where his body was most totally an icon for me was on our wedding night, and on the morning of his death. These two experiences are becoming more and more rare in today's society. Fewer and fewer people experience full knowledge of their spouse's body as late as their wedding night. I know that I was marvelously blessed. Some women have had horrendously ugly if not disastrous wedding nights. I had a beautiful one. It may be even more rare and unusual than I realize.

It is also becoming rare for a wife (or husband) to be with the beloved at the time of death. Because of this litigious society, hospitals are terrified of lawsuits if they don't keep the body caught in the dying process as long as possible. I have spoken with women who have done all the "correct" things, had "no code" put on their husband's chart, and yet the hospital has not observed these requests and has insisted on keeping the husband "alive"—which, since he is dying, is hardly the right word. It was both a wonderful and a terrible experience to be with my husband, touching his body with all the love of forty years of marriage, as he died.

This past winter I was privileged to be with an Episcopal nun as she left this world. She was in her eighties, had been vital and active and highly intelligent until her brain had the stroke that was killing her. She was an irenic presence in the Community, never able to take sides in an argument because she could always understand both sides. Her loving laughter often diffused tensions.

At St. Luke's Hospital, on the upper west side of New York, I was blessed to stand at her bedside in I.C.U. (completely against the rules, but with permission) with half a dozen of her Sisters, three of her children, one of her grandchildren, as Mother Madeleine Mary read the prayers for the dying. Each in our own way, we said good-bye as we prayed her out of this life and into another.

Then she was taken home to the convent where the Sisters bathed and dressed her, and her body was laid in state in the convent chapel while the Sisters kept vigil. The next day was the funeral—a real funeral, with the body right there in the chapel. We seem to be afraid of the word *funeral* nowadays; it is too potent a reminder of death. But this was a funeral, a true sending of a beloved friend to God, an honouring of her earthly body, and a giving of her wholeness to her maker.

And then, in her coffin, she was taken out of the chapel, down the stairs, out of the convent, and all of us present "asperged" her— splashed holy water on the coffin.

I have an image of her entering heaven, reaching down to hell and grabbing Satan by the scruff of his neck, then reaching for the Archangel Michael and saying, "All right, now, boys! What is this all about?"

There will be more peace in heaven because she is there.

Long ago I saw a photograph of Georges Braque and his wife as very old people, well up in their eighties, I would guess, and never have I seen more love in two faces. Their companionship is evident and beautiful. I said to my husband, "I hope that one day we will look like that." Perhaps my favourite picture of the two of us that I have on my walls is one taken about a year before Hugh's death, and there is love in that picture, too, love that does not grow up in a day and get cut down like a weed, but love that takes many years to grow and develop. And I am grateful.

The human body, that which Jesus honoured in his own flesh, can be a beautiful icon of the love of God, the body in its entirety, the eyes, the fingers, the toenails, the body hair—every single part. Paul affirms that the lowliest parts of the body are as important as those we consider the more "honourable." In our present culture we seem to be emphasizing the temporal at the expense of the eternal. Otherwise we might not be forgetting that our sexuality is not limited to our genitals. The touch of hands, fingers to fingers, can be full of electricity. A look, a smile, can convey as much energy of love as any toss in the hay—or elsewhere. But our emphasis is on sexual, genital fulfillment to the point where marriage vows have lost their potency, and honour is a forgotten word.

Our sexual desires have always been a double-edged sword. When they are conjoined with love they create great beauty and wonder. When they become things in themselves they can lead to disaster. We live in a society where we seem to have forgotten that.

Jesus was compassionate with the woman taken in adultery, but he also told her to "Go and sin no more." In our confused century it is often difficult if not impossible to differentiate right from wrong, but there is right, and there is wrong, and there is a choice between wishy-washy permissiveness and stony condemnation. But the balance is hard to find.

Would Mozart want to be remembered for his sex life or for his music? Is the question of whether or not Shakespeare was homosexual more important than the plays? The spiritual nourishment given by Rembrandt's paintings is what moves me, rather than curiosity about his sex life.

In heaven, Jesus said, there will be no more marriage or giving in marriage, no more worries, presumably, about sexual orientation. We will understand friendship in a new way.

There aren't any easy answers to the questions being raised today, and it may be too easy for me to remember Jesus saying, "Greater love has no man than to give up his life for his friend." Or wife, or children. Isn't staying with your family sometimes a real equivalent of giving up your own life? Cannot it sometimes be a blessing, especially if it is given with graciousness, not rigid rectitude? I believe that it can, because I know of families where this is what has happened.

Sacrifice is no longer popular, but I think that sometimes it can lead to true joy. Even the simplest of unions does not come free. There is always sacrifice. And sometimes that sacrifice involves keeping the marriage vows, those terrible promises of fidelity, for better, for worse, for richer, for poorer, in sickness and in health, till death do us part.

I know a couple in their late seventies who remind me of that beautiful photograph of the Braques, and whose love for each other lights up any room they enter. Their companionship is beautifully evident. They thrill to the same music, the same books, the same pictures. Have they never looked longingly, even lustfully, at anyone else? They probably have. I know that in my own marriage I was, several times, strongly attracted to men other than my husband. And he, surrounded by glamorous actresses, surely thrilled to their beauty. During Hugh's last months we talked about how grateful we were that neither of us gave in to those impulses. Yes, we had them. I think most people do. But we did not act on them. We do not have to act out everything we feel; that is idolatry of our own selves and does not lead to any kind of deep happiness.

I was blessed in my marriage with a husband I could honour, who took his marriage vows as seriously as I did. Many marriages are not so blessed; some marriages are not marriages at all and need to be dissolved. But, even in the dissolution, the icon of marriage can be honoured.

My granddaughters are sophisticated young women, New Yorkers, street-wise, not easily shocked. But they came in to my room one day with a copy of *Allure* magazine, and they were shocked. This is a legitimate magazine, read by many young women looking for beauty tips. It is neither cheap nor pornographic. But the full page, color, double-spread ad they showed me was. It was not only pornographic, it was full of terrible hate for women. On the right hand page a naked woman was depicted on all fours. On her belly as well as her pubic area she appeared to have teats. Beneath her, miniature men were reaching up as though to suckle. Her face showed a terrible grimace. Her head was totally bald. She was wearing stylish dark glasses—it was a while before I realized that the advertisement was for dark glasses. On the facing page two handsome young men and two women, all glamorously dressed, but all also bald, stood on marble pedestals.

It was indeed shocking. It was indeed pornographic. It was indeed idolatrous. What was going on? This was not a cheap magazine smuggled in the back of some "adult" book shop. (Why has "adult" come to mean pornography? What have we done to the icons of our bodies?)

Which came first, the chicken or the egg? Did the denial of the body follow the abuse, or is the abuse a result of the denial? Suddenly we are hearing horrendous tales of child abuse, by parents, priests, brothers, day-care center workers, male and female. Why are there so many reports of incest between fathers and daughters where the father is a rigid, Bible worshipping, fundamentalist Christian? The statistics are terrifying. Does the Bible condone this? One can pick passages out of Scripture that seem to encourage physical abuse. "Chasten thy son while there is hope, and let not thy soul spare for his crying. . . . Foolishness is bound in the heart of a child; but the rod of correction shall drive it far from him. . . .

Withhold not correction from the child; for if thou beatest him with the rod, he shall not die. Thou shalt beat him with the rod, and shalt deliver his soul from hell. . . . He that spareth the rod hateth his son . . . " and so forth. Proverbs is the easiest place to find these exhortations, but they are elsewhere, too. II Samuel 7:14: "I will chasten him with the rod of men, and with the stripes of the children of men." I Corinthians: "Shall I come unto you with a rod?" Hebrews 12:6: "For whom the Lord loveth he chasteneth, and scourgeth every son whom he receiveth." It is far too easy to misuse the Bible as an excuse for reprehensible behavior.

Has physical and/or sexual abuse always been going on, and we are just discovering what has been shamefully hidden? Or is there, indeed, more abuse as we stagger to the end of this sorry century? A little imagination, and a little sense of history, and the stories of other cultures, might put the brakes on here.

But there is a new atmosphere of attack, scapegoating, hate, that is worse than I have ever known it. One morning I looked up from my computer and out the window I saw a man throw another man against the hood of his car and beat on him. The street my window faces is a quiet street of white stone houses leading to the park and the river. I was totally startled at this violence. The aggressor got into his car, and the man he had just handled so roughly threw himself at the car, trying to get in. It was a large and heavy station wagon, and the man pushed at it, managing to rock it, but not overturn it, then climbed up on the hood and pressed his face against the window. I called downstairs to the doorman to ask him to see what was going on. My apartment is nine storeys above the street, and I could hear nothing. Almost as staggering as the behavior of the two men was that of the passersby, most of whom did not even glance at what was going on.

Perhaps I took this incident more seriously than I would have had I been down on the street, had I been able to hear what was said and see what was happening. Perhaps I took it more seriously because it was the end of a week of ugly, destructive hate. We live in an atmosphere of increasing racial tension, and because of an unnecessary misunderstanding, one day the tension in a local church erupted into violence, and I witnessed a mob in front of the church building screaming hatred and sounding, as I walked down the street towards them, like a film clip of one of the news reels of Hitler's Aryans screaming their hatred of Jews. Some of the people in the mob were the kind who enjoy joining mobs, but some of them were priests of the Episcopal Church, and as well as horror, I felt deep, overwhelming shame.

When there is a quarrel going on I usually ask, "Where would Jesus be?" And often the answer is, "With the people." But this time my answer is, "With the priest who was being attacked." I can almost hear Jesus saying, "I know, I know. I had the mob, too. They screamed 'Crucify him! Crucify him!' I know what it is like to be hated for the truth."

Jesus is the truth. Have we forgotten? What will make us remember?

Why is such violent hate getting worse? The irrational hate in front of the church made me understand that what has happened in Bosnia is not only possible in Bosnia and elsewhere, it is possible all over this planet. I had thought that after Hitler and the concentration camps such murderous racial hatred could never be acted out again, but I was wrong.

Surely the world is a terrifying place, but scapegoating is getting more and more violent, and it is probably even more evil because it does not realize it is scapegoating. Isn't this seeing the demonic everywhere a kind of demonic possession?

The reminder of the news clips of screaming Nazis caused me to question Christian hate—certainly a contradiction. If it is hate, can it be Christian? The psalmist talks about hating God's enemies with "perfect hate." One seminary professor remarked that it is quite easy to hate with perfect hate. Why is it so difficult to love with perfect love?

How do we prevent backlash? One of Satan's cleverest tricks is to move into something important and necessary and trivialize it. We are finally recognizing the horror done to the powerless, particularly women and children, in domestic abuse. This is too powerful, too important for the powers of evil to take casually, so in they come to try to undo the good that is being done in recognizing and trying to heal and prevent abuse.

My books about Vicky Austin and her family were recently re-issued in England. In *A Ring of Endless Light*, Vicky is at the burial of a close family friend, and she reaches out and holds her brother John's hand. Vicky is fifteen, John eighteen. In the new British edition she is no longer allowed to hold his hand. In *The Moon by Night*, Vicky, fourteen, has a date with a handsome but troubled young man. It is a traumatic evening for Vicky, and when she goes home to her aunt and uncle's house, her uncle is waiting up for her. He is deeply sympathetic to her pain, and there follows one of the key scenes in the book, as far as its "theology" is concerned. In the new British edition Uncle Douglas is not allowed to be in pajamas. "What!" I demanded. "At two o'clock in the morning? What do you want him to have on? Top hat and tails?"

Teachers or friends no longer dare to comfort and hug a small child who has fallen and skinned knees, in case of litigation. I received a letter from a young woman whose seven-year-old daughter had fallen down the stairs and bruised herself. The mother was afraid to send her child to school the next day in case of accusations of child abuse. A teacher who may have picked up a small child and cleaned off the knees likewise can be sued for child abuse in this hysterically and greedily litigious society—though many teachers, thank God, still hold and comfort their little ones anyhow. Touch is healing. We have discovered this in the church, where during the liturgy we pass the peace, and sometimes clasp each other's hands, or, if we know each other well, hug each other as we say, "The peace of the Lord be always with you."

But weren't we funny when we who are Episcopalian first started "passing the peace" in church! We tentatively held out our hands for a timid handshake. Some of us didn't touch at all, but made a grimace that passed for a smile. It was a while before we relaxed enough for the warmth that is common now.

But I heard recently of an Episcopal bishop who has forbidden his priests to touch anybody at the time of the peace—or any other time—for fear of litigation for sexual abuse. What are we coming to?

When I was young and working in the theatre and a man made improper overtures, I would just say, "Oh, bug off." I may have been lucky that nobody pushed it further, but a casual but firm rebuff worked well. It was, perhaps, a more innocent time.

And is the only beautiful body a young body? My husband at seventy was as beautiful to me as ever. My mother, in her late eighties, had a graciousness of body that comes only with age and experience.

Here is a true story I heard recently in Texas, about a beloved grandmother. One morning her young, pubescent granddaughter came down to breakfast wearing a see-through blouse. The grandmother said, "My darlin', you can't go out wearing that!"

"Oh, yes I can, Grandma," the girl said, and sashayed out.

The next morning the grandmother came down to breakfast wearing a see-through blouse. The granddaughter was shocked. "Grandma! You can't go out wearing that!"

"Oh, yes, I can, darlin'. If you can go out showin' your little rosebuds, I can go out showin' my hangin' baskets."

Yay, Grandma!

When the Second Person of the Trinity came to us as a mortal, he honoured our bodies forever, showing them as icons of divine love.

What has happened to us that we take our bodies so trivially, or so over-seriously?

I have worn my body for nearly eighty years, and I am comfortable with it. I would, given the choice, have made myself a beauty, but it's probably a good thing I was not given a choice. My parents in other ways were generous with their genes. I am grateful for my goodly heritage. As I grow older I want to continue to honour my body, to care for it, but not idolize it. I have been blessed with a husband who honoured my body, and with friends who love me just as I am, warts and all. We talk together around the dinner table and we wonder what has happened to escalate the warfare between men and women. And I think it is probably because we no longer see each other as icons, but as consumers.

We need to see each other as sacred once more, because God has made us, and what God has made is sacred.

5

JESUS

 Jesus should be for us the icon of icons, God sending heaven to earth, "Lord of Lords in human vesture." God has given us each other as revelations of divine creativity, and the ultimate revelation is in Jesus of Nazareth, the Incarnation of God into human flesh: carne = flesh. God enfleshed for our sakes. God's love offered to us fully and wonderfully and particularly in one person. But because it is impossible for our finite minds to comprehend that Jesus is wholly God, and at the same time wholly mortal, we try to prove the impossible, and that is to turn the mystery into an idol.

How much damage has been done—is being done—in the name of Jesus! How often it is done in the belief that God's will is being done! Jesus warned his disciples that people would kill them and think that such killing was doing God's will. How often have Christians killed and believed they were doing God's will! Alas, there are more examples than we can count; it is not only the Islamic terrorists who believe that God is pleased with killing.

And did God really want his people to slaughter *all* their enemies? After the Reformation, Catholics and Protestants killed each other with equal zeal, believing that they were doing God's will, that their way of expressing Christianity was what God demanded, and that those they killed were deluded if not downright wicked. But isn't that what Jesus refused to do?

Right now "Christians" are filled with hate as they eagerly look for things to condemn in other Christians, descending to malicious name-calling and angry accusations of New Ageism, or feminism, or even Satanism. Why are Christians afraid of one another? What—who?—has destroyed the love? What about the love? What about the love?

The Articles of Faith in the Episcopal Book of Common Prayer forbid us to believe in purgatory. (Obviously this prohibition was written before O'Hare Airport was built.) I find it a very comforting concept. Every time I have to change planes at O'Hare I say to myself, "This lets me off at least a day in purgatory."

This restriction was put in the Articles of Faith largely because purgatory smacked of Roman Catholicism. What is this terrible fear of the Roman Catholic Church which is found in so many Protestant denominations? Don't we worship the same God, the same Jesus Christ?

Yes, we do, I believe that we do, but not when we insist on a faith that is possible and provable. It is only by our icons that we are able to reach out beyond our finite limitations to the Maker of the Universe. When we ignore or fear our icons we, at best, trivialize our great holy days. Christmas! God, leaving power and glory and coming to live with us, powerless, human, mortal. What have we done to Christmas?

I love the Christmas tree (pagan though it may be), with the family gathering together to decorate it, but I wish that we were like the French (and many others) who do their gift-giving on Epiphany, with the coming of the wise men, and keep Christmas Day itself as a holy day. We forget the holiness and fall into sentimentality over the tiny baby in the stable. Who is that tiny baby? Even the Creator, almighty and terrible and incomprehensible!

Years ago, during the late sixties and early seventies, there was a short-lived "God is dead" movement in the church. I read some of the "God is dead" books, just so I could see what all the shouting was about, and afterwards my reaction was this: Gentlemen, I don't have your problem. Go ahead, do throw out the crotchety old man

you seem to have confused with God. But don't take my beloved
Lord away from me!

And I wrote a sort-of-poem, titled "The Baby in the Bath":

Throw out the bath water.
Never mind the baby.
The old man's made the water gray
and if we toss it maybe
we'll see God as we oughter
and all our fears will go away.

Throw out the bath water.
Never mind the baby.
I think he's dead already;
at least he's been forgotten.
The water's rank and rotten;
you won't get any thanks
if you rock the sinking boat
so steady, lads, steady,
if you hope to keep afloat.

Throw out the bath water.
Whoever is the baby?
Nothing but a little lamb
who says God is and that I am.
Catch the baby if you're able,
serve him up upon the table,
catch and kill the little lamb.
Garnish it and make it nice—
perfect for a sacrifice.

Throw out the bath water.
Who is this tiny baby?
Just an infant, meek and mild,
just a feeble, mortal child,

dying quickly, if not dead;
he won't turn your stones to bread.
Serve the lamb. We must be fed.

Throw out the bath water.
This babe can't help
so throw him out
otherwise he'll waken doubt.

Throw out the bath water,
never mind the baby;
throw the water, watch it flood
in the mingling of the blood.

Throw out the bath water
who is this tiny baby?
nothing but—run for your life!
the babe is sharpening the knife
angels crash across the sea
with flaming banner. Run! Oh, flee!
The trumpet blasts its brilliant notes
blown by wild and heavenly hosts
the red bath water's closing tide
will swallow all who do not hide.

Throw out the bath water
who is this tiny baby?
The Lord strong and mighty
even the Lord mighty in battle.

Run from the bath water
the Lord's alarm is sounded
run from the great avenging power
circled, cornered, utterly surrounded
you have no place to hide or cower.

> Throw out the
> run
> the king of glory's coming
> who is this
> even the Lord of Hosts
> This is the tiny baby!

Only that tiny baby, only the Lord of Lords, with us, truly, terribly with us, could bring us through the aweful events of his life and death all the way through to his resurrection and the glory of Easter.

Easter! When my children were little something told me that buying them Easter outfits to wear to church on Easter Sunday was idolatrous rather than iconic, and I made my girls, particularly, very unhappy by buying their spring clothes either well before or well after Easter, depending on where it came in the calendar. I think my instincts were probably right, though I was also probably quite unable to explain them so that the children would truly understand why they got their new clothes at a time that was different from their classmates. I was, I suppose, making a statement, and I was most likely the only one who heard it.

On our ship crunching its way through icy Antarctic waters we were all indistinguishable in our bulky red parkas. Although the penguins we saw varied in size and headdress, within their species each penguin was like every other penguin, male and female, all black and white and waddly and wonderful. They have no problem about Easter outfits.

After Easter comes a major holy day which is far too often ignored because it is too difficult to be contemplated rationally: the Ascension. There is something about the Ascension that I particularly love because it is so silly (silly used to mean blessed, in the same way that blessed is used in the Beatitudes). Jesus is standing with the disciples and suddenly he is "taken up," and they stand looking up into the sky after him, as though he were a hot air balloon, and two angels come and ask them why they are staring up into heaven. "He is not here," they tell the staring people, "but he's going to come again in the same way he was taken up."

Literalism here can cause a lot of trouble. A friend sent me a snapshot of a small country church, with a large sign outside proclaiming, "Sunday at seven thirty! Practise for the Rapture!"

How do you suppose a church full of people practise for the Rapture? Do they go outside and start jumping up and down, to see how high they can go? *Rapture* is not a word which will be found in Scripture. It is not there, no matter how hard anyone looks for it, and the concept of the Rapture seems to me to be a descent into literalism rather than an ascent into truth.

Jesus is constantly calling us to break out of literalism and into faith. Literalism puts what we believe in the realm of proof, and nothing I believe can be proved by theologian, philosopher, or scientist. It is faith alone that allows us to believe that the universe was created by a God of love, for a loving purpose.

We don't really know what happened at the moment of the Ascension, just as we don't know exactly what happened when Jesus left the tomb in which he had been buried. We do know that he was never recognized by sight, but only by voice, or in the breaking of bread, or the eating of fish. When the women told the men that an angel had told them that Jesus was risen, no one believed them. When Peter and John saw the empty tomb for themselves they just went away and didn't shout aloud to the rest of the disciples and their friends what had happened. We are not very good believers most of the time, we human beings.

Children are often better believers than we are. A young friend of mine who works in a day-care center one day overheard a little boy say, "I want to die," and he meant it. She swept him into her lap to try to find out what was wrong that he should feel and say such a thing (for her, the child's need was more important than worry that she might be sued for child abuse). Everything was wrong. His parents were drinking, fighting, screaming, throwing furniture. His anguish at the violence at home had focussed into a terror that someone was going to come take him away in the night. My young friend said to him, "I'm going to fix that for you. I'm going to send four guardian angels, one to stand at each corner of your bed. They will spread their wings around you, and you will be enclosed in their love, and no one will be able to take you away."

The next morning when he came to the day-care center she hurried to him, asking, "How did it go last night?"

He responded, very seriously, "I think we can cut down on the angel guard. One will be enough. The flapping of their wings kept me awake."

We lose that wondrous ability to believe in the inestimable power of love as we grow older and learn, often in brutal ways, that many people are unloving indeed, a realization which make us question God's love.

I am not sure what I believe about the Ascension. I try to understand it in terms of the culture of two thousand years ago when there were no planes, no helicopters, no space shuttles, none of the marvels which we take for granted today. If we were somehow precipitated back two thousand years and tried to explain to Peter, James, or John the ordinary world of today—showers, automobiles, television, smog, acid rain, jet planes—it would be far more difficult for them to understand that than something as simple as the Ascension!

It seems to have been a lot easier for Jesus' friends to believe in the Ascension than it had been to believe in the Resurrection. Maybe their acceptance of the marvel of Jesus' resurrection expanded their capacity for belief. Maybe it did look to them as though Jesus were wafted up into heaven. In a church in Greenwich Village in New York City there is an enormous painting of the Ascension behind the altar. All you see are Jesus' feet disappearing into the blue. Most of the other famous paintings of the Ascension show more of him than the feet, but they usually depict Jesus wearing a long white nightgown, floating up from the earth into the clouds. When the earth was smaller and time was younger and the universe was limited to what we could see, hear, and touch, the image of Jesus floating up into the sky was more possible to accept than it is now.

However the Ascension happened, what we do know is that Jesus did not want his friends to hold on to him. They were thrilled with the Resurrection body, once they recognized it to be the Lord, and they wanted to keep him with them forever. But he told them, in no uncertain terms, that it was better for them for him to leave them. He would send them the Holy Spirit; that was the promise. He would go, and then the Comforter would come.

How did they understand? When would they understand? Probably never completely, as we at our best do not understand completely. We need to move beyond the dominance of the intellect and understand with the spirit if we are to contemplate the reality of the Ascension. But we must also take great care that the understanding of the heart does not deteriorate into sentimentality and become idolatrous. With God's help it need not.

How do I understand Jesus telling his friends that it was better for them if he did not stay with them, it was better for them if he left them? I understand their wanting him to stay with them forever. Don't leave us! Don't leave us!

But he reiterated that it was better for him to go, that only then would he send them the Comforter, the Holy Spirit, the Third Person of the Trinity, the Person who is hardest for most of us to understand.

How could he leave them? He came, he was with them, he died, and then he came back to them. Transformed, different, but still recognizably their Jesus, the one who made life worth living. How could he leave?

When I think of those I have loved who have died I ask the same anguished question. How could you leave? How can the world exist without your living presence? It is outrageous that death should have taken you away! How can you not *be?* The old heavens and hells, heaven above, hell below, earth in the middle, make no sense whatsoever with our current understanding of the universe and the grandeur of creation. The old visions were believable when earth seemed to be all there was, the center of the universe and God's concern. Perhaps it was easier to comprehend death when all the answers were given, and descriptions of heaven and hell were taken literally. Life expectancies were far shorter than they are today, and people were frightened into being good because the tortures of hell were a continual threat. I suspect that true intimacy, true love, transcended this literalism, that when a mortal deeply loved another mortal, that love pointed to a God who loved them even more, not to a God whose love was so limited that he would toss people into eternal flames.

But what about now? Where, in the immensity of the universe is my husband? Where are my parents? Where are my friends who made such a difference to my life? Don't go! Don't go!

And yet, except for my own sake, I would not hold them back. I don't know where, in the gloriousness of God's plan, they are. But my faith is that they *are*, becoming more and more what the Maker wants them to be. It is not in the realm of proof, any more than Jesus' Ascension is in the realm of proof. But love does not vanish. Love is eternal, and whatever heaven is, it is in eternity, not time. Jesus of Nazareth left time and space, and the ascension is still hard for us to understand, so we don't pay as much attention to it as we should. The Holy Spirit came not only to comfort us, but to show us how to live in Christ, and only as we are in Christ can we begin to understand the mysteries of faith.

Most icons of the Ascension do not open windows for me, probably because I am letting literalism get in the way. Some icons will always be more illumined for us than others.

Henri Nouwen has written a beautiful small book called *Praying with Icons*. It is illustrated with four pictures of icons, and I looked carefully at the pictures before reading the text. The fourth picture is a head of Jesus, and he has his tongue stuck out in a delightful way, as though he is tasting something delicious. I thought to myself, "I wonder why Jesus has his tongue stuck out? Henri Nouwen will tell me." I read the book carefully and was startled when I came across nothing explaining Jesus' tongue. I looked again at the fourth picture, and finally I saw that what I had thought was Jesus' tongue was a stylized way of painting the lips, similar to lips in other icons. I was deeply disappointed. And then I thought, Never mind. For me, in this icon, Jesus is sticking out his tongue, tasting something wonderful, and calling me to that wonder.

Several years ago Simon and Schuster, the prominent publishers, asked if I would be interested in writing a text to go with the glorious paintings of the life of Christ by the fourteenth-century painter, Giotto.

I was honoured, challenged, thrilled, humbled. "Yes," I said, "I'd really like to try it."

The editor who had thought of the idea for this book took me out to lunch. "Now," he said, "we see this as a children's book."

"Halt!" I said. "Wait a minute! Think! Remember that Simon and Schuster was one of the publishers who rejected *A Wrinkle in Time* because it was considered too difficult for children. Don't you think children can understand the life of Jesus? Do you want it watered down? Made pretty? Do you want a book about a wimp? I am not interested." Finally I said, "Would you just leave me alone and let me write a book?"

And they did. I tried to write the best book I could, immersing myself in the magnificent paintings, plunging deep into the Gospels, trying to write with the understanding of the heart and mind together. We are never satisfied with what we have done. We know that our best is never adequate. If I had to be satisfied with what I have written I'd still be on my first novel. But I wrote what was for me the best book I could write at that moment in time. I thought I might get a lot of flack from the Christian literalists about this book, but mostly the ire of those who suspect my Christianity has been focussed on *A Wrinkle in Time*. A friend sent me an article from the *Washington Post* listing the ten most censored books in the United States. *A Wrinkle in Time* was one of them, and I felt very honoured, because it was listed along with books by writers who have been my mentors: Mark Twain, John Steinbeck, Teilhard de Chardin. But I was also deeply saddened. Are the censors (they are Christian censors) allying themselves with terrorists? If I believe that I am qualified to decide what the entire population of the United States, particularly Christians, ought *not* to be reading, am I not making an idol of my own judgment?

There are, alas, many books being published because they have enough shock value, enough unloving sex, enough perversion to ensure sales. Is one reason these books are being published the sad fact that books that call on imagination and compassion are being censored? I don't like a lot of the best-sellers, and that opinion is my privilege, but it is not my privilege to tell others they may not read them. Occasionally, out of a sense of duty, I will read a book I know the kids are avidly reading, to see what it is that is sweeping through their imaginations like wildfire, and I am sometimes saddened and sickened by the ugliness. I cannot say to the kids what I do not like about these books if I do not occasionally read one of them. The simplest thing I can say is that they are bad literature, that they see the human endeavor as being worthless, that they offer despair in a world crying out for hope, that they see condemnation in a world desperate for forgiveness and love.

Why are vampires so hugely popular in books today? Do they offer to their readers a promise of immortality that seems more real to them than that affirmed by a church which stumbles over the Resurrection? Are vampires taking up where the church leaves off? Satan quickly moves into such openings. I asked one vampire fan, "Is that really the kind of immortality you want? Do you want to live at the expense of someone else's life, someone you have to kill?"

"Well, but not all vampires do that."

"Yes, they do. There's no other way for a vampire to go on living but to drink a living person's blood."

Jesus did not drink other peoples' blood. He gave us his own—a very different thing. Would vampires be so popular if we remembered that?

As far as I know, none of these books is censored. It is extraordinary and tragic to me that many of the books on the censorship lists are the very books that proclaim God's love—God's inestimable love for all of us, not just for a selected few. Are we afraid of God's love? Is that why Simon and Schuster wanted me to write a life of Jesus for children, because they didn't think adults could cope with it?

One Monday afternoon at two thirty the phone rang. A man's voice said, "I've never read anything by Madeleine L'Engle, but you'd better turn on the radio to such and such a station, because nobody should be vilified on the air the way she is being vilifed."

I turned the radio on, to a "Christian" station. It was a very strange sensation to listen to a spewing out of hate, a septic vilification of me and of everything I believe. My response was instinctively visceral, as though someone were plunging a knife in my intestines and twisting it. I wanted my husband! I wanted to be held and protected from the violence of hate. Many of the accusations I'd heard before, but not on the air, not one on top of the other, with a few new ones tossed in.

What was coming over the air was hate, "Christian" hate, or at any rate hate that masqueraded as Christian, as I, and all my writings, were denounced as being not Christian, indeed, as being demonic. Is this hate what Jesus wants? Does the Lord really need to be protected from people like me? The interviewer mentioned another name, and the woman said, "Oh, we're going to get her, too." Get her? Is this what Christians are supposed to do? Get people? Not get them for Christ, but get them to destroy them in order to protect Christ!

Why is it a human tendency to enjoy hate, to be quick to believe anything evil that is told about anybody? Books of vicious gossip are often found on the best-seller lists, books that purport to be biographies of famous people, but which delve into as many ugly secrets as possible, particularly sexual ones, exploiting and sensationalizing them. Why do we want to believe evil of others? Is it that our own self-esteem is so low that we can raise it only by putting others down? We are none of us exempt from this virus, but if we truly hold to Christ's love we are helped to recognize it and combat it.

Were the words of hate pouring out of the radio pleasing to Christ?

It turned out that the woman, along with another woman, had written an entire book which was "out to get" me. The publishers were called and asked to send a copy. I am not going to mention the names of the book, its authors or its publisher, because I don't want to give that kind of hate any publicity or to demonstrate hate in return. The book denounced mythology, but the book's own title is from Greek mythology—an odd irony. As I flipped through the pages, every one contained a lie, a distortion, a false accusation. For instance, when Hugh and I lived in Crosswicks (our house, not a town, as the writers imply), we were deeply involved in the Congregational Church in the village; indeed, it was the center of our lives. According to these two women, we went to the Episcopal Church (there was none) and were atheists! I can't even call it twisting the facts because there were no facts. I was accused of levitating, of praying to a Buddhist statue, words taken out of context and distorted so that they were the opposite of what I had actually said—they were outright lies, in fact.

The women had evidently read my nonfiction book on story as truth, *The Rock That Is Higher*. There I tell about the accident that nearly killed me, and that in the ambulance and the hospital I held on to the ancient Jesus Prayer, "Lord Jesus Christ have mercy on me," like a sailor drowning in a rough sea holding on to the rescuing rope. According to these women, the Jesus Prayer is a mantra and is satanic. The name of Jesus is satanic? At that point I realized that I didn't have to read the book and join the women in the hell they had created, but I did have to take them seriously and pray for them with God's love, even when it is difficult to give them mine.

These women, like many of the attackers, call themselves fundamentalists, but that is not a good use of a perfectly good and useful word. I, too, am a fundamentalist, though the word is too often used pejoratively, to describe anybody who disagrees with a particular brand of Christianity. I believe the fundamentals of the faith. I get a lot of criticism from the fundamentalists, but God keep me from being literal about the literalists! I do care about the fundamentals, which to me are the rock of love on which I stand, the love that was great enough to create not only the magnificence of the starry sky but each one of us—the love that will never let us go until we become what our Maker wants us to be.

So yes, I think of myself as a fundamentalist, that is, someone who still cares about fundamental things, like truth and friends and imagination and love and story and honour and compassion, none of which seem important to the fundamentalists, or literalists, or whatever word we currently use. One can be a fundamentalist without being a literalist, and one can be a literalist without being a fundamentalist. It is when the two are combined that trouble is produced, so perhaps we need another word that is simpler than fundamentalist/literalist. A work like *fundalit*.

It is not only from the fundalits that such anger comes. The day after that radio program I ran smack against another instance of hate, a false accusation of sexual misconduct against a priest I know and trust. There indeed are horrible instances of sexual misconduct, but this accusation came from hate and a desire for revenge. What is there that makes Christians feel that hate can express the love of Jesus? Why are those who criticize my writing people who loudly proclaim themselves followers of Christ? Why do others, to my humble awe, find that the books lead them to Christ?

Perhaps I am wrong about not taking that book seriously. Several of my friends have read it all. I have not, because I do not intend to "do" anything about it. It is indeed libelous, but I don't want to meet hate with hate or even defensiveness (even though, like most mortals, when someone attacks me I tend to go into a defense mode).

Can one be a Christian with a heart full of hate? I know that when hate flickers in my heart Christ cannot come in. So, as I pray for compassion and understanding for myself, I pray for compassion and understanding for these poor women. If they deny themselves the richness of love, they are indeed poor! I turn back to my early prayer when my father was dying: "Please, God, do whatever is best for these two women. Only you know what is best. Please do whatever is best for them."

Hannah Arendt writes about "the banality of evil." When evil is banal, there is no sense of wrongdoing or guilt in the perpetrator. Surely many Germans convinced themselves that they were doing well in exterminating the Jews. Certainly these women think they are doing well in trying to exterminate me and all others like me—I am not the only target!

Psalm 56 is both comforting and cautionary. I quote here from the Coverdale translation, the one I use most often when saying Morning and Evening Prayer. "I will praise God, because of his word: I have put my trust in God, and will not fear what flesh can do unto me. They daily mistake my words; all that they imagine is to do me evil."

That's the comforting part. Yes, I believe that "they" mistake my words and that they quite apparently wish to do me evil. But then a few verses later I read, "Whensoever I call upon thee, then shall mine enemies be put to flight; this I know, for God is on my side." That is not comforting. Surely those Jew-hating Germans thought that God was on their side. There's always hate involved in war; that's one way patriotism is stirred up. We are the good guys, we're told, against the bad guys. The war against Hitler did not seem to be an ambiguous war, but how "good" it was I don't know. Certainly any civil war is ambiguous, each side believing that its side is God's side. But God is no respecter of persons, and God is always on the side of love.

Something else happened to upset me within the small period of time when I encountered so much hate. I was with a group of young friends, mostly from my church, who were born into and brought up in "evangelical" households. I did not grow up with their language, but I am now familiar with it, and I know that the particular people who came to my house that evening are strong with love and compassion and a willingness to listen to God and to change if that is what is asked. However, a college student who came by was not only turned off by the language of evangelical Christianity, but totally shocked at my friendship with people who spoke it.

Hey, wait! I thought. Not all Christians are bad guys! Have the hateful, hating Christians done such a thorough job of discrediting all Christianity? My young friend is a "cradle Episcopalian." Episcopalians do not use this language; we talk about using the right fork. (There is a story about three women who have died and who are in the waiting room to hell. They talk among themselves about why they are in the anteroom for hell, rather than in heaven. Mrs. O'Rourke sighs and confesses that she ate meat on Friday. Mrs. Cohen acknowledges that she ate bacon. Mrs. Courtney, the Episcopalian, says ruefully, "I used the wrong fork.").

I have become accustomed to the language of the evangelical world, and I know that my friends in the room that night were thoughtful, loving, forbearing, inclusive, not exclusive, deeply committed Christians. Their language turned the college student off not only because it was unfamiliar, but because she equated it with exclusive, hating, judgmental Christians, with fundalits who want hell heavily populated, who believe that a nuclear war can be won for Christ, and that God loves and will save only the fragment of Christianity worthy to be raptured.

So that was yet another shock, in a shocking fortnight.

John says in his First Epistle, "There is no fear in love, but perfect love casteth out fear; because fear has torment. Whoever fears is not made perfect in love. We love God, because God first loved us. If a man says, I love God, and hates his brother, he is a liar: for whoever does not love his brother, someone he has seen, how can he love God whom he has not seen? This commandment we have from Christ, that he who loves God must also love his brother," or sister. Or friend or neighbor. Or the two women who are so torn by fear that they write a book of hate and turn evil into such banality that the naming of the very name of Jesus can seem offensive to them.

Rabbi David R. Blumenthal in a lecture at Tulane University said: "Always, the same horrifying point: being good is conforming to the demands of a legitimate authority structure; morality is conscientious fulfilling of the expectations of a duly instantiated social hierarchy."

"Good" and "moral" Christians know exactly what the rules are, and any infringement, or seeming infringement, brings fear and its concomitant following attack against whoever has broken the rules or behaved in what is considered an immoral way. But what about Jesus? He knew what the rules were, and he cared about them; the law mattered to him. But when it was a question of love, love superceded law. He knew what morality was, and it mattered to him, but he cared more about love and repentance than legalism. Those Christians who are attacking other Christians are being obedient to an unquestioned authority and defining themselves and others by a rigid morality. Only Christ can free us from the prison of legalism, and then only if we are willing to be freed.

I don't want to lose the words *good* and *moral,* any more than I want to lose *fundamentalist. Good* can mean truly listening to God and trying to do God's will even when we know it may make us, at the least, unpopular, and, often, cursed. *Moral* can mean caring deeply about the needs of others, never ignoring those to whom wrong is being done, trying to do what we can do to alleviate the terrible pain in the world, not leaping into unthinking action but praying before we rush in, trying to understand what will really help rather than what will make us feel "good."

Far too often when we follow a course which we believe to be moral we will be going against the mores of the world, or what Walter Wink calls "the domination system." He quotes Ignatius of Antioch's *To the Romans:* "The greatness of Christianity lies in its being hated by the Domination System [world], not in its being convincing to it."

That is still true today. Isn't there a happy medium between moral rigidity and the pallid permissiveness in which nothing is forbidden and "honesty" means having your own way? One reason I was so horrendously shocked by the howling mob in front of that church was that they had joined the Domination System, and through it they were expressing their hate. So perhaps those who act from faith, like the priest who was being attacked, should not even attempt to be convincing to the Domination System. Perhaps my job with those who want to tear me and my works apart is to pray for them, not to try to convince or convict them.

Mary Magdalene is for me an icon of this kind of prayer, a woman hated by the Domination System, a woman who had been possessed by seven demons (they are never listed) and who had been healed by Jesus. She was the one to whom Jesus first appeared after his resurrection, and when she recognized him, she cried out, "Rabboni!"

"Rabboni" does not mean simply "teacher," as it is usually translated, but "my beloved teacher," a word of total intimacy, total acceptance of love, of wonder, of marvel.

I am not comfortable with a thin, legalistic, literal Christianity. Literalism did not help me when my husband was dying. It did not help me when a careless truck driver nearly killed me, nor during the long months and years of recovery. Literalism does not help me to hold up my body for God's love and healing. It does not help me in any of the perils or tragedies or joys of life. Literalism knows fear, but it does not know joy. And of course it permits no icons. Is the idea of a penguin as an icon shocking? Or the awesome and iconic beauty of icebergs and stone mountains?

The days between Ascension and Pentecost come in the spring in my part of the planet, when we are still bathed in the glory of Christ's rising from the grave, the glory of his once again walking the dusty roads of the land which he made holy, the glory of his breaking bread and eating fish on the shore with his friends. During the springtime it is perhaps easiest for us to contemplate such spring-like marvels as the Ascension!

Last May at Laity Lodge in Texas I heard a wonderful story of a little Mexican boy who entered first grade. He looked like a little old man, with calloused hands, and he didn't know anything, certainly not how to behave in a classroom, not anything. But he was quick and bright and eager to learn, and learn he did. After a while the first grade teacher began teaching the children about behaviour she considered appropriate, and behaviour which she considered inappropriate.

One day his little hand shot up. "Miz Clarke, djou know we is not supposed to behave wiz behavior which is inappropriate?" He had a slight lisp, so he pronounced it "inapwopwiate."

"That's right, Carlos."

"Djou know why we is not supposed to behave wiz behavior which is inappropriate?"

"Why, Carlos?"

"It'd tick Jesus off."

I told this story to a friend who is a retired archbishop. He said, "What a wonderful way to examine the conscience."

It is indeed.

In the evening when I read Compline, I ask myself what I have done during the day that would "tick Jesus off."

Then I move on to seventeenth-century Thomas Traherne, who believed that we are to give God pleasure, and I ask myself, "What did I do today that might have given God pleasure?"

That little Mexican boy with his intuitive understanding of the heart of the matter is an icon for me, an icon which is an open window leading me to Christ and to Christ's life in Jesus, and all the amazing mysteries which are part of the Incarnation.

Spring itself is so marvelous that it helps me to understand that Christ, the Second Person of the Trinity, came to earth as a human baby, lived as a human man—not a woman, a man. If you want facts, there's the fact. Jesus died on the cross, came forth from the tomb, and visited his disciples and friends at unexpected moments and in unexpected places, and then he left, and before he left they begged him to tell them when he would come again. He had already told them that he did not know, that even the angels in heaven did not know, that only the Father knows, but they were slow to understand, slow to accept what he told them (as are we). So they asked him again, and he told them, "It is not for you to know the times or the seasons; only the Father in the divine power knows this. But you (too) shall receive power, after the Holy Spirit has come upon you."

"What?" they wondered. Power? What kind of power? Power to overthrow the Romans? To free Israel? Roman power? No. No. How slow they were. How slow we are.

Power: the power of love, which is not dominance or control. Healing power. The kind of power that in the King James translation of Scripture is called *virtue*, thereby knocking over all our moralistic ideas of virtue. Virtue: healing power, not the world's definition of power. The world's definition is limited, overthrowable, prideful, unloving. When Jesus healed Mary Magdalene he removed the demons and filled her with virtue!

Shortly before the end of his time on earth, Jesus said to his disciples, "I pray for you, my friends, not for the world [with its worldly power], but for all of you whom God has given me, for you all belong to God. And now I am no more in the world, but you [the disciples, his friends, all of us] are in the world." God's world. God's creation. And Jesus continued, "I come to you, Holy Father. Keep through your own most holy name all those you have given to me [all of us] that they may be one, as we are One."

All of us, one with God, one with Christ, one with each other. We begin to get an idea of what this means when we think of the Body of Christ, and that we are each part of it, each an essential part; there is no part too small or too unworthy or too unimportant to be unnecessary! But it goes further than that.

"A new commandment give I unto you," Jesus said, "that you love one another as I have loved you."

To love one another as Jesus loved us. As Christ loves us. Can we do it? Can we love one another as Christ loves us? We have to. It isn't going to be any easier than trying to understand the Ascension, or the coming of the Spirit in tongues of flame at Pentecost.

God expects us to believe in the—not so much the unbelievable as in the unprovable, that which leads us into the glorious love of God.

Believing in the unbelievable is not believing in human constructs, like *Star Wars*, but believing in God's love, which surrounds us in all we do and at all times unless we reject it, or limit it. Even then, I suspect it is still all around us, but we have blinded ourselves to it. The Holy Spirit has come to help us to understand—the Comforter Jesus promised to send to us.

So must we. We must want to be changed by Jesus' marvelous act of loving, Christ willing to be Jesus, to live for us, to show us how to be human, to die for us, to rise from the grave for us, to ascend into heaven for us, to send us the Holy Spirit—and all for love. How splendid! It is so splendid that it cannot be understood by our finite minds alone; it cannot be understood literally. Literalism is death to Christianity, despite the protests of the fundalits, and we are left with Jesus' feet vanishing up into the air. The story is far, far greater than that. It is the truth we live by. It is glory!

6

AMMA

 Human beings have been making icons—and idols—ever since we got off all fours and became a two-legged creature, picking things up and looking at them, naming them, and naming each other.

On the way to Antarctica we stopped overnight in Santiago and went to a museum of pre-Colombian art and artifacts. There were many small figures of a woman's body, a body that was largely breasts and a full womb: an icon of fecundity in a planet that was sparsely populated. Life was precarious. Were there more births than deaths this year? Were human beings going to dwindle and die out, or would the birth rate manage to exceed the death rate? These primitive mother-figures were an affirmation of life in a world of violent death and, at best, short life expectancies. I doubt very much if they were worshipped as things in themselves. They were the equivalent for our ancient forebears of Marc Chagall's glorious windows, or Roualt's incarnational clowns—an effort by the human artist to reach towards the divine.

These little fertility figures are found throughout the planet, having been icons in all primitive cultures. Nor is the pre-Colombian museum in Santiago the only place where they are to be seen. Despite all our cultural and ethnic differences we human beings have much in common, including a need to make sense of our lives, our planet, our place in the universe. The mother-figures are part of our expression of awe, wonder, and worship. If they were worshipped as things in themselves, they would be idols, not icons. If I prayed to, not through, my icons, my Bible, any of my prayers, I would be idolatrous.

Throughout the centuries Protestants have misunderstood the practise of praying to saints and the belief that in heaven the saints still care for us, love us. We pray to the saints because we know them to be a living part of God's kingdom, part of that "great cloud of witnesses" who go before us. The statues in some of the churches are pretty bad art, which makes it easier to misunderstand. But if the prayer is *through* the saint, rather than *to* the painted plaster, then it is not idolatrous. In the Middle Ages many women turned to Mary because she was a woman like themselves, had borne a baby like any other woman. They could identify with Mary at a time when the divinity of Jesus had been elevated far above his humanity. The love of the humble, grieving mother was needed.

God as mother? Yes, of course. God as mother, father, sister, brother, lover, friend, companion. God as All, unlimited, unbounded, and undefined. The little fertility figures I saw in Santiago were reminders that these have been icons in all primitive cultures.

How much less primitive are we? Many magazines and papers come over my desk, and a recent one irritated me enough that I threw it out. I wish I hadn't. The lead article was to "prove" that it is wrong, if not sinful, to refer to God as anything other than Father. To call God mother, the writer said, is totally un-Scriptural. Any feminine reference to God in Scripture is simile, not metaphor. The world of Scripture is totally patriarchal, and we must not be tempted by the goddess religions which surrounded the ancient Hebrew and are menacing us today.

Well, yes, a lot of Scripture is patriarchal, and too often God is described as a tribal, warring God. But there's a lot of movement in the understanding of God between Genesis and Revelation. Are we supposed to stop moving? To stay stuck in the culture of several thousand years ago? To ignore all the discoveries about the universe that have opened to us a wider knowledge of its magnificence?

Should we go back to animal sacrifice and ask our clergymen and women to get out their knives so they can make wave offerings and heave offerings? Should we remind our priests to remember to smear blood on their ears and on their big toes?

And what about polygamy? Might that not be an interesting idea? Both David and Solomon had many wives. And should we, as the writer implied, put women back in their place, chattels, objects, possessions, inferior, unworthy?

What about this man who wrote the article? We're all locked into our own needs, held by our own bones and blood and hormones and hungers, our own opinions and prejudices. Can we ever let them go enough to understand each other? Or even enough to understand that there may be something to be understood?

God, the Maker, made us in the image of the Maker, and so we are Makers, too, as we struggle to affirm Creation in the making of icons.

There are times when I need the icon of God as mother. One of my favorite hymns is the ancient evening one, sung to the Tallis Canon:

> All praise to thee my God this night
> For all the blessings of the light.
> Keep me, oh keep me, king of kings,
> Beneath thine own almighty wings.

Night: the feminine, the enclosing, loving darkness of the womb, the preparation for birth. Light: masculine, where seeing is believing, and experiments are verified by laboratory testing, and concepts are worked out with intellectual vigour and humour. Night and Light, *both* needed, *both* beautiful, *both* iconic.

Despite the "King of kings," which is a masculine image, the comfort of being held beneath the wings of God is for me a mother image. Jesus, too, presents himself as mother when he refers to his longing for Jerusalem in terms of a hen brooding over her chicks. I need that motherly image of the protecting wings, almighty because they are protecting, rather than the other way around.

Perhaps this image is particularly important to me because at the time of my birth my father was still overseas in France, despite the fact that the Armistice had been declared and the First World War was officially over. When I was born my mother nearly died. She was so ill that she could not even give my name, which had already been decided on, so on my birth certificate I am listed as BABY. The earliest photograph of me is one of several babies in wire baskets on a hospital shelf.

I've had all the components of this memory for a long time, but for some reason I never put them together until after my seventieth birthday. That baby in the basket must have been fed, changed, kept clean, but I did not have that early maternal holding and loving and bonding that we now understand is all-important to the newborn baby. I'm not sure when Hannah came into the picture, our wonderful, loving Irish nurse, but it wasn't immediately.

Amazing and wonderful! I believe that God gives us our memories when we are ready for them. Why did it take so long for me to remember that as an infant I was, for the first few weeks, parentless? A temporary orphan? Maybe it was just as well. Might I have felt sorry for myself if it had occurred to me before? Now I can say, casually, "Oh, that at least partly explains why I am so insecure."

I have it in me to feel pity for that infant on the shelf in the wire mesh basket, but not self-pity. There is a difference.

A lot of work for people in therapy is the bringing up of memories that have been repressed. But I think there is a difference between a memory which has been repressed and one which has not actually been forgotten but has, for some reason, not been needed. I was not abandoned because my parents did not love me. I was very much a wanted baby. The circumstances of life simply prevented my mother and father from being near me during those early weeks when a baby bonds with the mother, especially the nursing mother, and in a different way with the father. At the point in history in which I was born, fathers still had little or nothing to do with their babies. They did not change diapers. Not many fathers dandled or held their infant children. I'm not sure whether or not mothers usually nursed their babies or whether the wet nurse had given way to the bottle. I do think that the sharing my husband and I did with our little ones was healthier and more normal than the practises which, in my mind, were "Victorian."

It is not only because I did not have the warmth of my mother's enfolding body when I was an infant that I need God as mother, the nurturing, forbearing, all-embracing mother who loves us, no matter what, who forgives us, no matter what, who affirms us, no matter what. When I am feeling down on myself, inadequate, clumsy, worthless, I need the mother to pull me onto her lap, fold the protective wings about me, rock me, tell me that it will be all right—perhaps not right now, not in human time, but in God's time. I need the Amma/God to rock me, to tell me that I am infinitely valuable, God's child, loved exactly as I am. I believe that we all have this dark underestimation of ourselves. Sometimes it is masked as arrogance, overestimation, superiority, but underneath the brashness the problem is insecurity and only unqualified, unmerited, unconditional love can assuage it.

Jesus called God Abba, Papa, Daddy, the familiar, comfortable name of love. Perhaps (would that we could ask Mary of Magdala or Mary of Bethany) he also called God Amma, Mama, Mommy, the familiar, accepting, nurturing name of love. Would we have fallen into all of those dreadful visions of the angry god, out to get us, lusting to punish us for our sins, if we had not limited our understanding of God to the patriarch—bearded, nightgowned, angry?

When we are infants our first love-giver is usually our mother. My mother was deprived of this joy by illness, but Irish Hannah, who somewhere along the line was called in to be my nurse, was a loving and mothering person. Nevertheless, like many of us, there are times when I search for this early, total love. Perhaps I passionately wanted to nurse my babies, in a day when nursing was not fashionable, not only because I thought it was the natural thing to do, but because my mother could not nurse me.

Nursing was total intimacy for me at a time when I had not yet had the chance to make the mistakes all mothers inevitably make sooner or later. Is the longing for Amma a longing for the perfect mother no human mother can be? When we look for this perfection in our human mothers, or in ourselves as mothers, we are making idols, not icons.

At a writer's workshop I was told a wonderful story about a two-and-a-half-year-old girl whose parents had just had another baby, another little girl. The parents had read all the right books about sibling rivalry and how to alleviate it. So when they brought the baby home and introduced the two sisters, the older girl was allowed to hold the baby, help change the baby. The parents did everything they could to keep her from feeling replaced or taken out of the spotlight or downgraded in any way.

At bedtime the parents spent extra time with the older little one, and everything seemed normal and happy until she said, "I want to see baby."

"Of course, darling. Come with Mommy and Daddy and we'll go see the baby."

"No. I want to see baby alone."

"Well, sweetie, Mommy or Daddy will go with you."

"No. I want to see baby alone."

And she was adamant. She wanted to see the new baby alone. The parents were understandably anxious about this request, but finally they decided to let her go in to the baby's room. There was an intercom. They could hear everything that went on. They could get there quickly if necessary.

So the little girl went, alone, to the baby's room, went up to the crib, and said, "Tell me about God. I'm forgetting."

Oh, someone! Tell me about God, I'm forgetting.

We do forget. We spend much of our lives forgetting, and instead of remembering we build golden calves: *My mother criticized me, no matter what I did. My father's expectations were too high. My sister was prettier than I was. They loved her more. I was not appreciated. Probably I was a changeling, and I got into the wrong family and my real parents would have treated me better. They would have understood me. They would have seen I needed special attention.*

Such thoughts are golden calves. Idols. Whenever we make idols we have lost the glory of the Creator whose messengers are angels, not golden calves.

Plato believed that all learning is remembering what we have forgotten. We have forgotten a lot. We've stopped believing in angels, and often we are hardly aware that we are worshipping golden calves. The paradox is that we try to turn angels into golden calves, or, more difficult and more frightening, we may discover we are under the influence of a fallen angel.

We all need Abba/Amma to love, understand, affirm us. Parents do. Grandparents do. Uncles and aunts and godparents do. Children do. It is a longing that is not fulfilled in this lifetime, because no mortal can give us the complete love our spirits need. Most parents do the best they can, even if it isn't adequate. Some parents are soiled souls who should never have had children and whose expressions of false parenting go from the extreme of child abuse to the opposite extreme of indifference.

Parents can also, usually unwittingly, be icons, icons of the love of God. I don't want to pretty up my childhood which surely was not the American norm. But my parents cared about truth, about honour. They were, in the wonderful, old-fashioned sense of the word, trustworthy. They were courteous. My father had a volatile temper which quite frequently blew, but then the sun came out, and there was no residue of cloud left over. You always knew exactly where you were with Father. There were no nursed grudges, no smoldering resentments. He did not carry around repressed anger. My parents by example taught me to love beauty, in nature, in music, in story, in painting. I might have been more lonely than is normal, but imagination was appreciated, not suspected. Perhaps some of my memories have come late because only now am I ready to allow my parents to be flawed and faulted human beings like the rest of us. And in their very flaws and faults they are, for me, icons.

What about Mary, the mother of God, as an icon? When I grew up in the Episcopal Church we didn't pay a great deal of attention to Mary, except in the "spiky" churches, which were "more Catholic than the Romans." We didn't exactly shun her, as part of popery, as many Protestant denominations did; we just didn't pay much attention to her.

In the Eastern Orthodox world she is known as the Theotokos, the most holy God-bearer and birth-giver. Perhaps the Orthodox have fewer false expectations of Mary than most of the rest of us do. And oh, yes, we do have false expectations of Mary, of our own mothers, and of ourselves as mothers, too.

Is there such a thing as a successful mother? I suspect that any mother who thinks she is a success is a manipulator.

Mary, the Theotokos, was not a success. The most spectacular thing she did was to say *yes* to the angel, an incredible response of courage and faith. She carried this extraordinarily conceived baby and she went, not to her mother, but to her cousin Elizabeth. What would her mother have felt about this heaven-sent child? Belief? Disbelief? Horror? Would she ask what on earth her daughter had been up to? Might her mother have wondered if it was some young man who had, perhaps, seduced her? Mothers are too close, too biologically bound to their offspring for any real objectivity.

Mary was young enough to accept the impossible. We tend to limit ourselves to the possible as we grow older. If Mary had the courage to take the impossible into her body, can we not have the courage to take it into our hearts?

Mary carried the amazing babe and went to her cousin Elizabeth, who could see things a little more clearly from the biological distance. Elizabeth, too, though past middle age, was pregnant, and that was another bond.

So what of Mary as Mother? We don't know a great deal. There have been arguments between Protestants and Catholics as to whether or not she had other children after Jesus. From the Gospels it seems apparent that she did. The odd problem for some theologians seems to be that they feel that Mary, after having given birth to the miraculous baby, should not have sullied her womb with other children.

Sullied? Isn't this a masculine, patriarchal way of looking at the whole glorious process of birthing? Is it an unacknowledged jealousy of a creative act from which men, by the nature of their bodies, are excluded? Does it partake of the old Middle Eastern fear of blood and the denigration of the feminine? If Mary had no more children was it assumed that she was perpetually celibate, never enjoying intercourse with her husband? Scripture said that Joseph "knew her not" until after Jesus was born. Then, I hope, Mary and Joseph were able to fulfill their love for each other, to enjoy each other, to know each other. Mary, the perpetual virgin, never menstruating, never reaching to her husband in love, is as unreal to me as the pictures of an emasculated Jesus who could not have lifted a hammer or a saw.

Scripture mentions brothers and sisters, and there's a tradition that Jesus' brother James was one of the disciples.

After the Annunciation and birth we don't know a great deal about Mary. She and Joseph took the infant Jesus to the temple to the high priest with the appropriate offerings, and two very old people recognized him, two people so old that they, like the very young, were able to accept the impossible. It is interesting that our capacity for belief is greatest when we are children and when we are old. I find it far easier to believe God's glorious and impossible (not literal) actions now than I did when I was in my middle years.

Ancient Simeon warned Mary that a sword was going to pierce her own heart, and after he had seen and held the baby he was ready to depart this life in peace. His song, known as the *Nunc Dimittis*, has been part of the Vespers or Compline service since the very early days of the church.

Mary scolded Jesus when he was twelve. He'd "tarried" in Jerusalem (while his parents were returning home after the feast), lingering to talk with the temple "doctors," priests, theologians. And his parents did not understand him.

How many parents understand their twelve-year-olds?

How many twelve-year-olds understand their parents?

His first miracle was in a sense pushed on him by his mother. She has rather jokingly been referred to as behaving like a typical Jewish mother in this scene. Jesus had just started his public ministry. He and his disciples arrived a little late at a wedding feast given by friends of the family. His mother rushed up to him, telling him, "They're running out of wine." Obviously she wanted him to do something about it.

This story is only in John's Gospel, and as I reread it, Jesus sounds impatient with his mother, if not downright cross. He is not yet ready for miracles. He says, "Woman, what have I to do with you? My time is not yet come."

Despite this put-down, Mary, amazingly certain, orders the servants to do whatever her son tells them to do, and he turns water into wine, and fine wine at that.

After this we see little of his mother during his grown-up life. The three synoptic Gospels all mention Jesus speaking to a gathering of people and being told that his mother and brother (and sisters?) are looking for him. And Jesus gives the seemingly chilling response, "Who is my mother? Who are my brothers?"

His mother and his brothers have come looking for him at a time when he has already become a threat to the religious establishment of his day, with his loving and forgiving God, Abba, Papa, instead of the god of domination who controlled people through fear. Jesus had presumed, himself, to forgive sins. He had broken the law by healing on the Sabbath Day. He'd told fascinating and very pointed stories. He had preached the Sermon on the Mount which turned the usual way of looking at things upside down. As he himself remarked, he was becoming a prophet not without honour—except with his own people, his own family.

Why were his mother and his brothers asking for him? Probably to beg him to quit this foolishness which was becoming a public scandal and come home.

This reminds me of the elderly woman who went to her travel agent and asked for a ticket to Nepal. The agent said, "Lady, I'll get you a nice round trip to Orlando and Disney World." But she wanted to go to Nepal. So, reluctantly, the travel agent ticketed her. She went first by plane, then by train, and then by bus. Then by donkey cart, then by donkey, and finally on foot. It turned out that the reason she wanted to go to Nepal was to see one particular holy man who lived at the top of one of the highest mountains, and she was determined to get there.

As she walked the last few miles she was told that the holy man was there, but that he saw very few people, and she would be allowed only three words.

She agreed. That would be satisfactory. She made the last half mile on her hands and knees and came to the top of the mountain where the holy man was sitting in his saffron robe with his shaved head and rice bowl.

She crawled up to him and said, "Sheldon, come home."

Mary loved her son, but she had more or less the same attitude: "Come home, Jesus. Stop parading around like a prophet. You're upsetting the authorities and embarrassing your family. Stop this nonsense and come home."

Like almost everybody else, including his own disciples, Mary did not understand her son, or what he was about. Nevertheless those words of his must have cut her to the quick. She was beginning to understand what old Simeon had meant when he had warned her that a sword was going to pierce her own soul.

But worse was yet to come.

Jesus did not come home. He continued to teach, to heal, to tell stories. His friends were all the wrong people. He had women for close friends—unheard of! He took water from a woman, totally taboo. He took water from a Samaritan woman, a double taboo, and yet this woman was one of three people in the Gospels who recognized and affirmed Jesus as the Messiah: Peter, Martha of Bethany, and the Samaritan woman at the well. One man, two women.

We have heard Jesus' stories so often that we tend to forget some of their sharpness. Almost all of the protagonists of his parables are outside society, Samaritans, lepers, a Syro-Phoenician woman, quarreling brothers, blind or maimed men. (If you were blind in those days it had to be your "fault.")

Did Mary, his mother, have any idea what he was talking about? Did she remember the shepherds and the Eastern kings and the great gifts? Did she remember the years in Egypt, and the terrible price paid for Jesus' life, in the death of all those little ones under two? Maybe it was all too strange and terrible for her to dwell on overmuch.

We don't see her again until the crucifixion.

And then the sword went all the way through her heart.

A mother waiting for her son to be crucified. My imagination rips like old cloth. I think of mothers with sons on death row. I think of a friend who rocked her dying little boy for over a week, rocking and singing "Something Like a Rose" to him until he died. I think of mothers receiving phone calls of accidents, mothers waiting in hospitals. There is an ache in my sternum that I cannot describe.

Mary was there while her son was dying. She was not alone. There were other women with her. And there was John, with whom she would spend the rest of her life which, according to tradition, was long. Jesus spoke to her from the cross, and speaking from a cross demanded great and terrible strength, because crucifixion was largely death by strangulation, with the lungs collapsing and the heart laboring with congestive failure. But Jesus spoke to his mother and his friend, the only one of the disciples to be there in his final agony.

And John took Mary home with him.

She is not mentioned in the Gospels after the Resurrection. It may have been another piercing of the sword through her heart too terrible to bear to see the resurrected Christ and not see him as her human son, Jesus. The risen Lord was never recognized by sight, but she would have known him in ways too deep for sight, or sound, or even touch.

She had held his dead body. As far as we know, she never held the risen Lord. But of course we don't know. What happened to the women, even the woman who gave birth to the Messiah, was not carefully recorded. Much of what we know about Mary we know only by myth and tradition and story. She wasn't a great success as a mother but, like most of us, she did the best she could within the limits of her understanding, and that should give us all courage, whether we're parents or not. We don't have to succeed in our relations with parents, children, friends. We do have to do the best we can, without putting false expectations on ourselves.

Mary loved her child. She rocked him and nursed him and played with him and laughed with him and scolded him and let him go. She let him be God, and that, too, must have been a sword piercing through her heart. Could we do that, any of us human mothers, let our baby go that far away from us, further away than we can even begin to imagine? She let him be God, and so with courage even deeper and stronger than giving Jesus to us by birthing him, she let him go completely in order that all the rest of us should know the risen Christ.

7

ABBA

Abba.

Abba, Daddy, Papa, Father. Because so much emphasis in the past has been placed on the male aspect of the Creator, I've considered Amma, the female aspect, first. But to leave out Abba is as much of a fragmentation as leaving out Amma. Both are anthropomorphic, human attempts, because we are human, to see God in terms of ourselves. Amma is not the correct word for Mama in Hebrew, but it is simple, alliterative, and works for me. Would that I spoke Hebrew, but I don't. I'm not carelessly being inaccurate; in English Abba/Amma sings itself iconically in my heart.

Abba and Amma know each other, love each other, create together. It takes both to make the image of God, as is made very clear in Genesis. When we refer to the "image" of God we refer to both male and female principles uniting, two making one. It is an image of love and creativity. What have we done to it?

It is not only the secular world that has male and female constantly fighting, disagreeing, denying each other. But all creation comes from the joyous intercourse between male and female—not rape, but love; not lust, but sharing; not grabbing, but true, joyous giving.

What are some Abba icons? Again, the penguin, specifically the Emperor penguin, who incubates the eggs which the female penguin lays on his feet. He covers them with a flap of abdominal skin and stands there, during the entire time it takes the babe to come out of the shell, fasting, losing half his body weight in the process. Only when the egg is hatched and the female returns does the male Emperor rush into the sea to find food. What a lovely, sacrificial icon.

In the early societies when human beings were just beginning to make pots and pans and weapons and little images, like the fecund mother images we saw in Santiago, the masculine images usually mightily magnified the phallus, again the image of fecundity, pro-creation.

In those early days the sun was worshipped as male, the moon as female. Fire, perhaps, was a male image, water a female one, each essential to creativity, to planting, to growth. Jesus reminds us that the seed cannot grow unless it is put into the dark, into the ground, to die to itself as seed before it emerges into the light as plant or tree or flower.

The images of lord and king have been smirched by what human lords and kings have done with their abuse of power, giving Lord Acton cause to write his famous, "Power corrupts. Absolute power corrupts absolutely."

That has been our history as mortals. Our faith, on the other hand, is that God's power is unlike our power because God's power is incorruptible, and that is at least partly because God is servant as well as lord, subject, but never object.

How? Through the Incarnation. We refer to Jesus as the Son of God. Jesus always referred to himself as the Son of Man—one of us. He emphasized over and over to his disciples, who were, one and all, caught up in the power game, that the Son of Man came to serve, to be the servant of the people he ruled. If the disciples were slow to understand, so are we.

At the time of the Last Supper, Jesus enacted this servanthood in washing his disciples' feet. On Maundy Thursday in my church we wash each other's feet, taking turns. After your own feet have been washed, you then turn to wash the feet of the next person. To me this is deeply moving and beautifully symbolic. Some people find it hard, too hard for their participation, so they draw back. In my church we make it clear that it is optional. To most of us it is a deeply moving privilege. Some of our parishioners know that this may be their last Maundy Thursday on this earth. It is a deep honour to wash the feet of someone who, like Jesus, is near the end of this mortal journey.

But despite Jesus' warnings of his approaching death (murder), the disciples were still obsessed with power, arguing about who should be first among them. They had heard Jesus' many parables which pointed out his understanding of servanthood, of humility. "When you go to a party, don't take the best seat, in case someone more important than you comes in and you have to move. Instead, take the least important seat, and then perhaps the host will tell you to come up and sit beside him."

Icon. As the Risen Christ sitting at the right hand of the Father is an icon.

In Jesus' time the women prepared the feast and served it, but did not sit with the men. How very different from my own table, where Hugh sat at one end, I at the other, with our guests between us. There was no particular head nor foot; I sat at the end nearest the kitchen for convenience sake, because of the two of us I was the one who enjoyed cooking. It wasn't like that in Jesus' day. Women served. (So why shouldn't they serve at Communion, at the Lord's own table?)

Jesus was a man. A servant figure, a son figure, but not—to me, at any rate—a father figure, and this is probably because of his own emphasis on his heavenly father, his own insistence on his sonship— his sonship of us mortal creatures.

Too often the images of the Father have been of an old bearded man, wearing a white nightgown and scowling at creation, as though he didn't approve of what he had made. Disapproving, as though he had to be placated for his mistake with creation, particularly creatures. But this was not the heavenly Father my parents taught me when I was a child, and I am grateful to have been taught about a God who made me and loves me just as I am.

And it is this loving Father who guides my life and whom I encounter in my own quiet prayers, and in church, and with my prayer group. And even in my writer's workshops!

One of the joys of writer's workshops is the stories that come from them. Let me share two, written by the same person, a retired Episcopal priest. The first is a new version of the creation story. As of now, the general opinion of the scientific world is that everything started with what is familiarly known as The Big Bang. After The Big Bang the voice of God was heard saying, "Whoops!"

The next story was a second assignment. Often for a first assignment I will ask the writer to turn to Scripture, look up a story about a woman at a time of decision and conflict, and write a story about her. The next assignment is often to take the story and hand it to the person sitting on your left. That person is to rewrite the story from the point of view of somebody else in it. So this was a second assignment from a story about Hannah, the mother of Samuel. This writer chose four different points of view. He wrote brief monologues from the point of view of Eli, the priest who was given the child, Samuel, to educate; from the child, Samuel, himself; from Elkanah, Samuel's father; and finally, from the point of view of an angel.

The angel says, "Oh, God, please don't send me back to earth again. It's just terrible. What can I do with these people? Please don't make me go back again, please! . . . What? I don't have to go? You mean it? I don't have to go? Oh, thank you, God, thank you! What? What? You mean—you're going?!"

Even the angel was surprised.

God!

God coming to earth! God, caring enough about us recalcitrant creatures to come to us!

It used to be taught that God has no need of us, that God has no needs at all. It also used to be taught that God is our parent. Two contradictory points of view! If children have need of their parents, the parents also have need of the children. My children are grown and out of the nest, and I try not to interfere, but I am still part of their lives, even from a distance. I need to be in touch, by phone, and as often as possible in person. I need to love them. I care what happens to them.

It is my belief that God cares what happens to creation and all that that happens to every single one of us who has been made. I don't really think that God said "Whoops!" What I believe God said is, "It is good! It is very good!" Even after he had made the human beings who were going to betray him over and over again. Judas's betrayal of Jesus is the one we focus on, but it began with Adam and Eve.

There's a story that when God made Adam he looked at him and said, "I can do better."

But did he? It seems to me that we all trip over pride, arrogance, resentment, fall flat on our faces, regardless of whether we're male or female. And God still cares about us, loves us enough to come to us, as one of us. God is here, with us, part of the story, all through Hebrew Scriptures. In ancient thinking an angel was not only an aspect of God, an angel was God. When Abraham was speaking with the angel about the fate of Sodom and Gomorrah, suddenly he is speaking to God elself: "Shall not the Maker of the Universe do what is right?" Bold talk, wasn't it, but Abraham had learned to be secure in God's love.

Today it seems to me that there is a great deal of insecurity about God's love and a great fear of God's anger. Surely we give God cause for anger, but I think again of my husband and myself as human parents. Sure, occasionally we got mad at our children, but Jesus said, "If your child asks for an egg, will you give him a scorpion? And you're only human parents. How much greater is my father's love for you!"

We human parents love our children as best we can, and though it's often not enough, far more often we're grieved, rather than angered, when they do something they should not have done. I suspect we grieve our heavenly parent more often than we anger him. "My children, my children, how could you have done this? How can you behave this way?"

When Adam and Eve listened to the tempter, rather than to God, God came after them in the cool of the evening, calling for them. "Where are you?" Where are you? God asks of us when we turn away. Where are you?

Sometimes we reply, "I'm here. What is it?" And often we are reluctant. Moses stuttered and tried to get out of doing what God asked of him. Gideon said, "You can't mean me!" Isaiah said, "I am a man of unclean lips." Jeremiah said, "I'm too young." The only one I can think of offhand who said *yes* immediately was Mary. When the angel came to her with his incredible demand, she replied, "Be it unto me according to your word." Mary had total faith in God, and in God's Word, and faith that God's Word was Love. Could anyone who did not believe completely in God's Love have given birth to all Love, God come to us as Jesus?

God almost always asks the impossible. If it is possible, if it is easy, we can almost always be sure that it is the Tempter asking, not God. God asked Abraham to leave his comfortable home, long after reitrement age, go to a strange land with his wife, who was long past child-bearing years, and start a family. He asked Gideon to free his captured people from a vast enemy, far more powerful than the little group of Jews hiding in the mountains. He asked the prophets not to foretell the future, but to tell the people where they were, right then, where they had gone wrong, where they had stopped listening to the God of Love, and how they had become, most of them, far more secular than we are in our secular cities today. And he asked Mary to give birth to Jesus who was going to save us from ourselves and our sins.

And Jesus? What did God ask of Jesus and who was Jesus? Jesus was God, for starters. If our Christianity is Trinitarian, we believe that Christ, the Second Person of the Trinity, left the Godhead to come to us as a human being, to live with us, to show us what it is to be human. If we are Trinitarian Christians we are asked to believe that Jesus was totally human and totally divine and that, of course, is impossible.

Yes, once again, God is asking the impossible. We can be reluctant. Throughout history most of God's chosen people have been reluctant. We can say, "It's impossible!" and turn away. We can, as some Christians have done, emphasize the divinity of Jesus to the exclusion of the humanity, and we can, as other Christians have done, emphasize the humanity at the expense of the divinity. It's lots easier. But God doesn't ask the easy things. Satan does. When Satan was tempting Jesus after his baptism, all the temptations were for Jesus to take the easy way out. And Jesus, being fully human and fully divine, refused Satan's wiles. God does ask the impossible. And with God's help, we can say with Mary, "Be it unto me according to your Word."

When I am in a quandary about something, I usually ask, "What would Jesus do?" And often I don't know the answer. Life is very different at the end of the twentieth century than it was two thousand years ago. But I know that whatever Jesus' answer would be, it would be the loving answer. And love, like Jesus, is seldom easy. When it's easy, it's sentimentality, not love. Love often says *no* when we would like the answer to be *yes*. Jesus did not allow all the people he had cured to follow him as one of his disciples. He told them to stay where they were and spread the word of love, and often they were disbelieved. He didn't let the rich young man come to him, keeping all his riches. Whenever Jesus calls us, something has to be given away. Our self will. Our eagerness to make judgments about other people's sins. Whenever I do that, I can almost hear Jesus telling me to look at my own sins, instead.

We're living in a judgmental era, particularly in the church, pointing fingers at other peoples' sins, and some of them have sinned indeed. But what about mercy? Several years ago I was speaking at an Assembly of God college in the Midwest, and during the question-and-answer session one young man stood up and said, "Your books really do indicate that you believe that God is forgiving."

"What an extraordinary statement," I responded.

"No, no," he contradicted himself. "What I really mean is that your books do seem to indicate that ultimately God is going to forgive everybody."

I give my best answers when I don't have time to think and get in the way. I heard myself saying, "I don't think God is going to fail with creation; I don't believe in a failing God. Do you want God to fail?"

"But there has to be absolute justice," the young man said.

"Is that what you want?" I asked. "Absolute justice? You're maybe nineteen or twenty. If you should die tonight, wouldn't you want at least a tiny little bit of mercy? Me, I want lots and lots of mercy. Don't you feel the need of any mercy at all?"

That had not occurred to him.

And mercy, like love, is not easy. As one of the characters in my new novel says firmly, "Mercy and permissiveness are not the same thing." God's love is totally free, and if we accept this gift it is also totally demanding.

So, do I understand the Incarnation? Of course not. I live by it, but it is far beyond my finite, human comprehension. Scripture tells me that it is God loving us so much that he sends his beloved Son to us for our salvation. It is an ultimate act of love on the part of the infinite God. It is when we insist on understanding the Infinite that we get into trouble, trouble that caused the crusaders to slaughter Greek Christians, that a few centuries later caused the Inquisition, Christians burning Christians, and a few centuries later caused Catholics and Puritans to murder and destroy each other because each one thought that his group had *the* truth and the other group was absolutely wrong. It is when we insist on defining God's love or God's anger that we blunder into antisemitism or join rigid sects which promise us all the answers.

God did not give answers; God gave himself, to save us, to free us from our sins. When Christ was born as Jesus in a barn in Bethlehem, that tiny baby bore our sins, and he bore them all his life as he grew into manhood. How heavy they must have been during his last weeks on earth when he knew that his dearest friends did not understand him and were going to betray him. How heavy they must have been when he hung on the cross. But for love of us he carried them. How blessed we are in his love!

Why can't we remember that his last commandment was that we should love each other as he loved us? John, in his first epistle, tells us firmly that if we cannot love each other, love the people we know and have seen, we cannot love God whom we have not seen! If we are able truly to love one another, then we will get a glimpse of understanding of the magnificent love of God.

A comprehensible, anthropomorphic god has never worked for me, not even Michelangelo's magnificent fresco. I "see" the Father by attributes, rather than visually. Because I am human, some of these attributes are those of my own father: the integrity, honour, bravery. Not the outbursts of anger that came from the fierce pain in his mustard-gassed lungs, his career cut off at its height, so that he could no longer travel all over the globe as a foreign correspondent when travel was far more challenging and dangerous than it is today. But the fortitude, yes, and the refusal to wallow in self-pity, and the self-less and realistic anguish at the clouds of another war looming ever more darkly on the horizon.

God, too, must be anguished at what has been happening in his creation, what his creatures have done. The Old Testament is full of war images, and glorification of war. These images are singularly lacking in the words of Jesus; oh, yes, there are a few, but what comes over most clearly is the call for us to be human, to be loving, to be open to God's revelation.

From my Abba God I want truth, understanding, absolution. Not only forgiveness of sins, but wiping them out. We used to talk about the remission of sins, but that word has lost its original meaning because *remission* has now become a widely known medical term. When cancer is in remission there is no promise of total assurance that it will never come back. The cancer is gone for now, but may not be gone forever. Whereas, when we talked about the remission of sins, they were gone, as though they had never been. That is what happens when God forgives our sins—the whole Godhead, Father, Son, and Holy Spirit—God sharing in the anguish of the terrible end of Christ's mission on earth.

We all sin; we all wound Jesus; we all cause God pain. We need help. Nowadays we tend to talk about spiritual direction rather than confession. ("Spiritual direction? Confession?" someone asked. "Isn't that New Age?" I doubt if the New Agers are particularly interested in looking at their sins before God and praying for their forgiveness.) Spiritual direction does not necessarily include confession, though confession does include spiritual direction. Are we afraid of the word *confession?* Are we afraid to admit that we have done something wrong and that we need to confess it and be forgiven? The marvelous thing about sacramental confession is that when absolution is given by the priest as God's representative, the offense is wiped away. We are not to dwell on it any more, but to go on afresh with our lives, knowing ourselves forgiven, restored, loved. My tendency has often been to go back to and dwell on my mistakes, but my confessor—and I am glad that Tallis was my confessor as well as my spiritual director—taught me not to go back and play in the garbage. Let it go. Get on with your life, understanding that God has wiped out the sin. And what God has wiped out we may not take up again, otherwise it becomes an idol.

In the current Prayer Book the absolution given at the end of the confession in the offices of Morning and Evening Prayer is this: "May the Almighty God grant us forgiveness of our sins, and the grace and comfort of the Holy Spirit," leaving out the two phrases which used to go in the middle: "true repentance, amendment of life." This is a dangerous omission. Unless we are able to repent, able to struggle, with God's help, to amend our ways, we are subhuman.

There is the story of the young monk who goes to his abbot and begs the abbot to forgive him for his sins. The abbot replies, "What sins? You'll have to remind me; I've forgotten."

What Abba has forgiven we must learn to forget, too. To let go, to wipe out. Clean the slate. Start a new page. Use whatever metaphor works for us the best.

There's the story of the man whose wife nagged and nagged him for some past mistake until he cried out in frustration, "But I thought you said you'd forgiven and forgotten."

She replied, "Of course I've forgiven and forgotten. I just don't want you ever to forget that I've forgiven and forgotten."

Is it Abba who forgives our sins? Or Amma? Or both of them together, lovingly, tenderly?

Abba/Amma. Papa/Mama. Elohim. Plural. God who transcends our anthropomorphic imagery in total love. The One who loves us enough to say *no* when it might be easier to say *yes.*

What about the great Creator, the Maker of the universe? The universe is enormous beyond finite conception, both macroscopically and microscopically. How can one Maker keep track of it all? How do I pray to someone who is so great and grand and glorious as to be able to fling suns across the sky and yet note the fall of every sparrow, number the hairs on our heads?

I still pray as I did when I was a child, to the God of Love who knows me, inside and out, who knows the depths of my heart, who knows every one of my desires, great and trivial, and from whom no secrets are hid. I still pray to the God who is great enough to become small, to become human, so that I can know, in my limited finitude, what unlimited, infinite love is like. Often it is too much for me. I am caught up in attacks of reason, in hurt feelings, little vanities, angers, exhaustion. I get in the way. But somehow or other Love always manages to be there when I let down, to encourage me when I am afraid of the dark.

And there are times when I am afraid of the dark. I get in a shadowy place of over-exhaustion of body and spirit. Sometimes physical problems overwhelm. My old knee that has troubled me for most of my life continued to deteriorate, and finally it was decided that I needed a new knee, an entirely new knee. I went to Crosswicks for Christmas, and on the twenty-eighth of December Bion and Laurie drove me to New York, to St. Luke's Hospital, for surgery the next morning. I said to the surgeon, "I don't want general anesthesia. I don't think it's good for the elderly brain."

He replied, "The medical profession is beginning to agree with you. I will use an epidural block."

I am grateful for that, and for the care I got in the hospital by doctors and nurses. For the loving concern of my friends. Each evening around eight o'clock two of the sisters from the Community of the Holy Spirit came and read Compline, the beautiful, evening office, with me. Various priest friends brought me communion. I was in the hospital eleven days, and on the eleventh my friend Marilyn, from Niles, Michigan, came to help bring me home from the hospital, and then she stayed with me and nursed me for three wonderful weeks. They were, yes, wonderful. Marilyn, who has been a friend of the heart for many years, had come to me in the hospital in San Diego, and now she was with me again, nurturing, caring, full of compassion and fun. We laughed together, prayed together, reading the strong and affirming words of both Morning and Evening Prayer. And, yes, there was a lot of pain, but I was so surrounded with love that it was easily bearable. Friends came to help with the cooking, the cleaning, to visit, to have fun. It was probably the most sociable winter I have ever had! As soon as possible I got back to the stove, though those who stayed to eat also stayed to do the dishes. I got very spoiled.

Since I was homebound and could not travel, I offered a writer's workshop to the parishioners of my church, and every Tuesday evening during February and March a group of delightful young people came to my apartment with their writing, and they did some really exciting work.

Winter was long and cold. I tried to resume a reasonable schedule, but New York had an inordinate number of blizzards. It was, in fact, the worst winter on record, and when there was ice outdoors I didn't dare go out in case I fell and crashed onto my new knee. I began to feel weary with frustration and continuing pain. Surgery wallops one's mind and spirit as well as one's body.

I had planned to do a great deal of reading and writing during the period of recuperation. This didn't happen. One of my friends said, "Madeleine, all your energy is going into your knee." And I think that was so. I worked hard at the exercises the physical therapist gave me, and that was the largest part of my work. When it snowed he warned me, "Madeleine, don't you dare go out. The orthopedic floors of the hospital are jammed. You must not risk slipping on the ice and falling on your knee." New York had seventeen major blizzards, so I was housebound a lot of the time.

But at last spring came to this hard city. The dark and ugly bushes on the islands of upper Broadway suddenly burst into the glorious blooms of magnolias. Tulips, daffodils, cherry blossoms. And yet my heart continued to be dark and wintry. Then suddenly one morning I woke up singing in my heart, "When morning gilds the skies, my soul awaking cries, may Jesus Christ be praised!" And I was ready, eager to greet the day. There was no reason for this transformation. Sheer grace. And my heart soared with gratitude.

And I am reminded that this magnificent Power loved us enough to give us the Mystery of the Word Made Flesh. Abba, Amma, loving us enough to come to us. I do not understand this love, but it is what keeps me going. If I had to understand this love, it would stop being love and become idol.

The penguin, wobbling its clumsy way down the rocky hillside and into the rough, icy water, does not understand the glory of this sudden freedom in the buoyancy of an element which has less gravity than air, but this lack of conscious understanding is part of its value as an icon.

8

STARS

 My first remembered icon was a heavenly one indeed. It is so important to me that though I have written about it before, I cannot leave it out here. I was a very small child visiting my grandmother at her beach cottage in north Florida. One night someone came into my little room, untucked the mosquito netting from around my crib, and carried me out onto the beach to see the stars. It must have been an unusually beautiful night for someone to have said, "Let's wake up the baby and show her the stars."

All I remember is glory.

There were no nearby city lights on the horizon to dim the magnificence of the night. The stars patterned the sky with their heavenly dance. The wind was quiet, and the ocean rolled gently to the shore. The little waves lapped the sand, and the lacy froth picked up the starlight. It was my first glimpse of night, of the world that was far larger and more magnificent than the ordinary daily world of the small child. I have never forgotten that moment of glory. When I am sad or depressed, or when all that I believe seems too great to be believed, if I can go outdoors and see stars I will be pulled back into proportion. I am part of all that has been made, and rather than feeling lost in insignificance I feel great joy to be even a tiny part of creation. When I look at the sky I am looking not only into vast areas of space, but also of time. There are galaxies beyond galaxies, not only far beyond the range of my naked eye, but beyond the range of our most sophisticated telescopes. When I can get up to the country, to Crosswicks, I can stand out in the yard, with the dogs rushing around chasing each other, and look at the stars, and I can see a star that is seven light years away, and a star that is seventy light years away, and a star that is seven hundred light years away, and seven thousand, and seven million, billion, trillion . . .

In Antarctica I missed the stars. It was still full daylight when I went to bed. What the stars there must be like in winter I cannot quite imagine, because they must be more glorious than stars at home, even in the country, where lights from cities fifty or more miles away still dim the skies. My grown children have remarked that the stars around Crosswicks are not as magnificent as they used to be, when we could see the great river of the Milky Way flowing across the sky. There are more lights now, city limits have spread along with the population. Even so, on a still, cold night the stars are radiant in their glory, and I have the extraordinary privilege of seeing vast reaches of time as well as space.

One of the reasons space travel is impractical is that time increases with distance. If someone from Alpha Centauri, seven light years away, should be able to look at our planet at a twelve-year-old girl, the observer would be seeing a five-year-old girl, seeing, as it were, backwards in our time. Since most stars are much further away, the observer might be seeing her great-great-grandparents, or even further back to when people lived in caves or trees, or even further back to when our solar system was being formed . . .

We can't begin to comprehend. Perhaps I'm less bothered by this mathematical astonishment than I would be if I'd ever paid much attention to numbers. But I haven't. It seemed to me somewhere along the line that I had to choose between words and numbers, and I chose words. It also happened that I had very bad teachers in the grades when the foundation of arithmetic is given a child, so I never got this foundation. I am in awe at the immensity of space and time, but I don't feel I have to understand either one. As long as the One who made them understands, that is enough.

That icon of the glory of God's Creation is, in a way, the answer to all the unanswerable questions about the creation of the universe. Time! Where in Genesis do those magnificent opening phrases mention that God created in human time? God created time, but Scripture makes it very clear that God's time is not our time, that a thousand ages for us are less than the blink of an eye for God.

As long as creation has a Creator, can't we leave the mystery of time to this great artist? As for space, it is as mysterious as time. Scripture warns us that we are not to worship the stars; that would be to make idols of them. But to see God's work in the stars, to see God through the stars, is something else indeed. Far too many people have deprived themselves of rejoicing in the heavenly bodies as icons by assuming that they are idols, but idols are always things-in-themselves. Not icons! When we worry about worshipping the stars we forget their Maker. The Creator delights in our rejoicing in Creation, rejoicing, and never forgetting that the stars are signatures of the Maker.

I have been asked, "Aren't you being pantheistic?" Don't you see god or gods in everything? Isn't that tree-spirit god? Aren't the stars gods or goddesses?

No! If that's how it was for me, that *would* be pantheism.

But to see God, the Creator, in all of creation, is quite different. In books by Matthew Fox and John Polkinghorne the word *panentheism* is used to differentiate it from pantheism. We see God's signature in all of the wonders of creation. In my own acts of creativity, in my stories and poems, isn't my signature there? They are not me, though they tell a great deal about me. And because I believe in my stories, that they are gifts to me from the Holy Spirit, I want to share them. Artists want their paintings to be seen, their music to be heard, their words to be read. If I turn on the radio and tune into part of a symphony, I can usually make a pretty good guess: Oh, that's Mozart. Or Beethoven. I walked into a small church in Barcelona, and there was a large painting, and I cried out in surprised joy and recognition, "El Greco!"

So, I believe, God wants us to rejoice in the great work of the universe. God's Creation tells a great deal about God. One of my favourite moments in the turning of the seasons is very early spring, when the daffodils are opening their sun-bright blossoms, but when the trees are still bare. Yet when we look at them against the sky their sharp lines have softened. They are not ready to leaf out, but their buds have changed the lacy pattern to a misty gentleness. Smaller trees and bushes are already green, but the great trees are opening more slowly to the spring. This brief time of year is one when I most clearly see God's signature.

My granddaughters and I took bread and cheese and fruit and a bottle of wine to Riverside Park where we spread out an old blanket and picnicked, watching the river and the sunset through the lacy branches of budding trees, showing a soft tracery against the evening. We ate and watched and talked of deep, heartfelt things, and sang and laughed and relaxed until dark, and it was a foretaste of the heavenly banquet.

From the library of the Cathedral of St. John the Divine I look across the Close through the flowering fruit trees to the great bones of the cathedral. They are most beautiful in the winter, when the trees are bare; as the sun sets the windows on the south turn into diamonds. When the sun goes, the stone picks up the light and breathes with pastel color. In the spring the trees are leafed, and I can no longer see the stone through the green. Winter or summer I am worshipping neither the cathedral building nor the budding trees nor the flowers. The beauty is simply a marvelous relief in a dirty city; here I can see God's signature rather than that of the creature who too often forgets beauty in favor of a utilitarianism which will bring in more money. Utilitarianism can be beautiful, too, but unfortunately, it often isn't.

As I sit at my desk in my New York apartment, about a mile through the streets of the Upper West Side from the cathedral, I look down the street, past the trees of the park, across the Hudson River, to New Jersey. My window is large, and I have a view of the sky with its infinite variety. Sunsets over the Hudson are one of New York's greatest beauties. I love seeing boats moving on the river by day and by night. After dark I see the lights across the river, and the lights of planes flying from the south and west to LaGuardia Airfield. I can see a few stars, but not many, because the city lights are too bright. Last spring a series of very bright lights appeared in

New Jersey at the right side of my view, and they were so brilliant that I thought they had to be for some important scientific laboratory at the very least. It turns out that they are the lights for a golf driving range. They go off at eleven, which is a mercy, but the city lights still keep the heavens too bright for stargazing.

In the winter when the bitter cold freezes the river, from my desk window I can see great ice floes, and by them I can tell which way the tide is flowing. When the floes move majestically up the river, the tide is coming in. When they glide down the river the tide is going out. These floes are miniature versions of the ice floes I saw in Antarctica and again remind me of the wonder of creation.

Seeing God in and through the stars, or the great ice floes, or the lace of tree branches against a wintry sky, is not pantheism. It is rejoicing in God's signature. It is being aware of God's hand in all that is made, even in the things we think we have made, such as the apartment buildings I also see from my windows, or even the small trees my fellow apartment dwellers and I have planted in front of our buildings. I often long for stars when I am in the city.

After I graduated from college and moved to New York, to Greenwich Village, far downtown from where I am now, I was so lonely for stars that I would take the subway uptown to the Planetarium. There are not many places left where we can see stars in their full glory as I did at the beach when I was a baby. Sometimes in a plane at night, flying high above the earth, we can glimpse the glory of the heavens. At sea, especially on a freighter, where there are no lights of discos and other amusements for the passengers to dim the night, we can see stars.

One of my favourite places on the planet is the conference center, Laity Lodge, near Leakey, Texas. It is one of the most beautiful pieces of earth I know, and it has become my pattern to go there once a year for two working weekends and have the week in between for myself, an uninterrupted time to pray, to write, to *be*. Usually my friend Betty Anne Cody is with me, also taking *being* time. We pray a lot, we laugh a lot, we talk deeply of questions both private and cosmic, and we already have a tradition of driving away from the Lodge, which means driving for several miles in the Frio River, along its shallow limestone bed. This past spring as we were gently swishing through the twilight waters we came on a great blue heron. Betty Anne stopped the car about three feet from this great bird, and the river continued to swirl around the wheels of the car as we gazed, awed, at the heron who paid us no attention until Betty Anne turned on the headlights so we could see better, at which disturbance the beautiful creature quietly flew away. We continued along the river, then up the banks, up a steep road, and on to the highway that led us to Leakey where we headed to our favourite local truck stop for a TexMex dinner.

After we have feasted we head for the lodge, stopping on our way back to look at the stars. Leakey is several miles away from the entrance to the lodge; there aren't any lights to blur the sky. The stars blaze at us in nearly primeval brilliance.

When my Florida friend, Pat, comes to Crosswicks, the old house in northwestern Connecticut that is so dear to me, we often tramp across the fields and through the woods to the Star Watching Rock and stretch out on stone still warm from the sun, our home star. There, as night falls and the other stars appear, we, too, talk as we have talked since we were gawky teenagers, and conversation under the stars tends to have an added depth. Now that Lyme disease is a very real threat (my doctor daughter-in-law has treated a goodly number of cases), and people with no spleens are warned to be particularly careful about ticks (my spleen had to be removed after the automobile accident), we are more apt to sit on the terrace under the night sky than to tramp through bushes and brambles to the Star Watching Rock, and that is a loss, but a sadly realistic one. So the great flat rock is now more an icon in memory than in present actuality.

But one of my joys in bed at night if sleep is slow to come is seeing in my mind's eye the places which have been icons for me: my grandmother's beach cottage, long gone; the tiny train winding at night like a golden dragon down the mountainside in Switzerland; the "mountains of the moon" in Guelin in China, and many, many more.

Sometimes I have been alone watching the stars, and sometimes I am blessed by their crystal chiming, by the heavenly music of the spheres. We no longer listen enough, we over-civilized human creatures. If we can quieten ourselves, hush both our inner and outer worlds so that we can listen, God has much to tell us through Creation. It is not surprising that when God wanted to speak really seriously to Abraham el took him out under the stars. "Count the stars if you can." And of course we can't, and that's part of the marvel of it.

When I was a child, and an adolescent, visiting my grandmother at the beach, after the evening meal I would leave the rambly cottage and the world of grown-ups and walk past other cottages until I came to a wide, high space of dunes. I would climb the highest dune and lie there on the golden sand listening to the ocean breathing deeply, and waiting for night. In North Florida the sub-tropical night comes with startling suddenness. There is a brief moment of pearly twilight and then night comes, and suddenly there is a blaze of stars.

At least that is how it was, then, in my early adolescence. Now the dunes are gone. The cottages are gone. A change in tides caused by over-building has narrowed the beach. There are motels and hotels and condos and at night electric and neon lights dim the stars.

But in my memory it is still wild and wonderful. I am wearing shorts and a cotton shirt and my feet are bare. I lie on the sand which is still warm from the sun. With night a slight breeze rises and the steamy heat drifts away. The glory of Creation is above me. This is the place where, as a baby, I was first shown stars. This is the place where I first had an awareness of the marvel of creation and the Creator. I was a mere speck in this immensity, but I did not feel dwindled. Instead, I felt a part of all that has been made. I rested in God's love.

Amma, Abba. The sand beneath me held me warmly in a maternal embrace, protecting me as I watched the heavens. The stars are my first icon, a special gift from the Maker.

Now when I visit my friend Pat and ask to go to the beach so we can splash in the little waves as they move in to the shore, so we can see the dunes laced with scuppernong grape vines, or crowned with sea oats, we have to go to one of the state parks, the only land in that part of North Florida which still looks as it did when I was a child. It is a terrible loss.

If I worshipped the stars as things-in-themselves they would be idols, and I an idolater. But the stars are far more than things-in-themselves; they are affirmation of the glory of the Creator; they are affirmation that all matter matters, and that this mattering is most profound in the Incarnation, the baby born in Nazareth, of a human mother, as all babies are born, and who is the greatest icon of all.

Yes, I need icons. I think we all do. Anything we can say about God is inadequate. St. Augustine said, "If you think you understand, it isn't God." When we think we understand we plunge immediately into idolatry, into a god we have made up to suit our needs. Oh, yes, it is true: A comprehended God is no God.

I look at the stars and I do not understand. But I *know*. I know, not with my mind, but with my heart. The Maker of the stars made me, made each one of us. We are loved, and what is expected of us is that we return that love with love.

It is not difficult to understand that our forebears, living on a planet that was sparsely inhabited, generally as ruthless as Antarctica is today, and with far many more predators, would need a god who was mother, protector, birth-giver. It is easy to understand why they would worship the sun, the moon, the stars. The rhythms of the earth were ordered by the heavenly bodies, which surely appeared to circle the earth. When boats were built, sailors learned to guide themselves by the motions of the stars. Crops depended on sun, on rain, on darkness and light. While worshipping the heavenly bodies may be pantheism, ignoring them is ignorance—are we not ignorant when we ignore? God sends us messages through all of creation. One of the great insights taught us by today's physicists, with their much greater sophistication about the nature of creation than was available to the early humanoids, is that all of creation is interrelated. What happens to the smallest subatomic particle has its effect on the greatest galaxies. In a cosmic sense, all actions have consequences, the actions of human beings, of tiny insects, of ocean waves, of distant galaxies.

We know that we are deeply affected by the moon; the tides move to the pull of the moon. Men's bodies, as well as women's, have their lunar cycles, though it is more apparent in women. It is because of the moon that our own planet is as stable as it is in its turning on its axis, in its journey around the sun. The moon is of just the right size and density to hold us steady; without it we would oscillate so wildly that more or less stable seasons would not be possible, and life as we know it would never have come into being. It is the moon's beneficence that keeps our planet on course.

A cousin of mine who worked in a mental institution said that at the time of the full moon, patients who ordinarily were allowed to use knives and forks became potentially violent and had to have them taken away. This is where the word *lunatic* comes from.

The moon affects us. The stars affect us. This is far more compatible with Christianity than it is with the New Age! But we are so put off by those astrologers who use their gifts, real or imagined, to make money, that we shrug off what is real as well as what is phony. The magi who came from far away to see and worship the child Jesus knew how to read the stars. In our insistence on having all science, including astronomy, be in the realm of proof, we have lost much of what those ancient astronomer/astrologers knew. Through the world of particle physics, the study of particles so much smaller than the stars that they are hardly conceivable, we are beginning to return to that knowledge which does not ignore proof, which works hard for proof, and then goes beyond it.

We tend to look down condescendingly on the early dwellers on this small planet because they worshipped the sun, the moon, the stars. We, of course, have changed as our knowledge has been enlarged. But how much have we actually changed in our understanding of God? Wouldn't you think that when, back five hundred or so years ago, we learned that planet earth is indeed not the center of the universe, but part of a much greater whole, our concept of God would have grown along with our knowledge? But has it? Don't many people still think of us as the center of everything, particularly God's interest?

Haven't we learned that God is not the anthropomorphic God of our ancestors, that God is so great and wondrous and awesome that any description is inadequate? Perhaps the simplicity of our forebears who lived long before there was a written language has something to recommend it. We are small and God is great. Perhaps the one valid thing which has been affirmed and reaffirmed is that God is love. That is enough.

Despite our assumed sophistication we are still superstitious creatures. In the dark, strange January of 1993 my granddaughters and I turned on the television to see if there was anything worth watching and were caught by the predictions of astrologers for the coming year. The predictions were all dire. It was going to be a terrible year. They were not wrong in that. The year was a difficult one, no doubt about it. But all the psychics who were interviewed in that TV program predicted that there was going to be a major, disastrous earthquake, probably in California, in April or May. Now 1993 is over, and most of their other dire predictions were equally wrong. My granddaughters and I agreed that it is not good to put only negative expectations on the people who turn to TV for edification and entertainment. When we are told everything is going to be terrible we are likely to believe it, and it becomes a self-fulfilling prophecy. I remind myself that God made the moon and the stars, and that God made a universe where there is free will. Actions do have consequences, but the consequences are not set in cement. Some wrong actions can be redeemed; some wrongs can be redressed.

It used to be believed that events in heaven were enacted in a smaller way on earth. I'm not sure what that means, but it does *not* mean that everything that is going to happen in the rest of this year is not only predicted, but set. We do not live in a predetermined universe. What we do does make a difference to the future. Even the smallest acts of love can make a difference.

Yes, I do believe that the heavenly bodies affect us, the sun, the moon, the planets, the stars, the galaxies. Our radios and TVs react to sun flares, and so do the instruments of ships and planes, and so, in all likelihood, do we. What is now popularly called PMS is certainly affected by the moon. The effect of the planets, of the stars, is less easy to detect, but there are probably times when our tempers, and those of the world's leaders, are more likely to flare, times when we—and they—are more likely to be reasonable. But we do have control over our tempers, our reasoned actions. Let's not abdicate!

Of all full moons, the Paschal full moon seems to be the most potent. I am not sure why, except that perhaps the entire planet is holding in memory the terrible events of that week which led to the cross and then—alleluia! to the Resurrection. At the great cathedral where I work, and down the street at my parish church, I see this. Great churches seem to attract troubled people, and people who are mildly troubled can become wildly troubled during these days between the Paschal full moon and Easter; I've seen it happen.

On the occasion of the last Paschal full moon I had an errand in mid-town New York, the area of the city which used to be called the Great White Way, the world of theatre and music, but which is now shoddy and dirty and full of movie marquees proclaiming pornographic or "adult" films and other obscenities. On one corner stood a group of three or four people, one of whom was preaching—shouting—about hell and damnation, and weeping and wailing and gnashing of teeth. I said to the friend who was with me, "I can't stand it. If they're still here when we finish our errand and come back, I have to speak to them."

How totally unAnglican of me! On our return they were still there. It was the day of the full Paschal moon. I went up to them and said, "Please. You should be telling people that God loves them!" I pointed to the people walking by, most of them looking beaten, or depressed, or belligerent. "Please tell them that God loves them!"

One young woman said, "If they don't accept it, they are damned to hell."

"How can they either accept or reject God's love if you don't tell them about it?"

"They're *bad*."

"Probably. So all the more they need to hear about God's love for them! Tell them! Tell them Scripture says that God so loved the world that Christ came to live with us, to be with us, to show us that wondrous love. Tell them!"

I was met with blank stares.

I wonder if I'd have done that if it hadn't been for the full moon? UnAnglican or not, I don't regret it. Obviously, at the moment God's love meant nothing to these street corner preachers, who cared more about getting people into hell than into heaven. But maybe, later on, maybe that night when they were perhaps praying quietly—who knows?

They reminded me of a preacher who was preaching to his congregation about hellfire and damnation, weeping and wailing and gnashing of teeth. One old woman protested, "But I don't have any teef."

The preacher bellowed, "Teeth will be provided!"

I heard that story from gentle Brother William in a monastery where I was giving a writer's workshop. That evening the last Scripture reading in chapel was one of Matthew's more gory passages about hellfire. I went to bed and to sleep and I dreamed. Jesus came and said, "No, no, you have it all wrong. You don't burn away the sins, you wash them away with pure, clear water, very, very gently. You must be *very* gentle! And if the sins are deeply ingrained, you wash them away with warm, soapy water, very very gently."

I woke up in the morning and breathed, "Thank you. Thank you."

What is it that the two-and-a-half-year-old girl wanted her baby sister to tell her about God? What was she in danger of forgetting? God's inestimable love.

I went home from Forty-second street and Broadway and the hellfire preachers and thought about the days of Holy Week that lay ahead of me, the days of the passion of our Lord, and it came to me very clearly that the real passion came long before the cross. In a sense, we pay so much homage to the cross that we forget when the sacrifice began.

In my mind's ear I can hear God saying to God, "Can I do it? Do I love them that much? Can I leave my galaxies, my solar systems, can I leave the hydrogen clouds and the birthing of stars and the journeyings of comets, can I leave all that I have made, give it all up, and become a tiny, unknowing seed in the belly of a young girl? Do I love them that much? Do I have to do that in order to show them what it is to be human?"

Yes! The answer on our part is a grateful Alleluia! Amen! God so *loved* the world that he sent his only begotten son . . .

That is part of my story, part of the story that a lot of the world, even the Christian world, has forgotten. We have allowed Satan to trivialize Christmas into greedy sentimentality. But it is awesome, awesome. No matter how the story of Christmas is told, it is a story that is beyond the limited realm of provable fact. We cannot prove in any lab or university or seminary classroom that the power which created the universe, all the galaxies, all the stars in their courses, limited that power, totally limited it to the unknowing of a zygote, in order to become one of us, in order to show us mortals how to be human.

"Tell them that God loves them," I begged those street corner preachers. "They need to be told that God loves them." We all need to know that God loves us. I need to know. You need to know. We all need God's love.

So I went home and back into the darkness of Holy Week.

The time of the full Paschal moon is soon over. Easter will come and we can cry with joy, Christ is risen! He is risen indeed!

Do we truly remember what that means? Do we truly understand what has been called the greatest story in the world? Not when we are more interested in damning people to hell than in getting them into heaven. When we forget God's love and concentrate on God's anger, aren't we becoming idolaters?

Or, if we want a God we can prove, or an Incarnation we can prove, aren't we making an idol, rather than falling on our knees in awe of the wonderful mystery? It's a lot easier, a lot safer (in finite terms) to worship an idol than to expose ourselves to the fire of the eternal God—not the flames of hell, but the flames of love. Perhaps that's why some of the best theology is found in story—Jesus' stories, the stories of Daniel or Gideon or Esther or Jael; the novels of Dostoevsky, the plays of Shakespeare, the stories of O. Henry; and—yes—stories written for children. Not so much myths or fairy tales which were originally not written for children, but *The Wind in the Willows* or *The Book of the Dun Cow* or *Grandfather Twilight* or *The Secret Garden* or (of course) *Alice in Wonderland* and *Through the Looking Glass*. That's why some of the theology that matters to me most is in my fantasies.

Children need their comforting icons, the blankie, the stuffed animal. Perhaps the little fertility goddesses, usually small enough to hold in the palm of the hand, were equally affirmative to our ancient forebears. I, too, need my Amma icons, and I have many, long-loved, cherished ones—icons, not idols. In my living room is a large painting of my great-great-grandmother and my great-great-great aunt. One is holding her flute, the other her harp. They lived in Charleston, South Carolina, and they understood story and honour, even if their understanding was very different from ours. If they had been born a few generations later they would not only have educated their slaves, which they did, but they would have understood that slavery is intolerable. Perhaps they understood without realizing it that when they provided education the people they educated would understand quite clearly the sinfulness of the system in which they lived.

But slavery was nothing new when it came to the American South. Understanding that it is evil came very slowly to the human being; it was simply taken for granted throughout the ages, including the time when Jesus walked the earth. Paul advised his slaves to be obedient and their masters to be considerate. But my female forebears were strong in thought for their time. I admire them, and I do not want to let them down.

Sometimes at night when I am in the country and can see the stars in their full glory I think of these women, and that they looked at a night sky that was not very different from the one I am seeing. When a star is a few million years away, a couple of hundred years doesn't make much difference.

When I am able to be in the country, at Crosswicks, the electricity is volatile. My son told me on the phone one day that he drove up from the nearby town, stopped in at the local store, and found it dark. "Is the power outage general?" he asked, and was told that it was. "What caused it?" he asked. Someone grunted and said, "Tree damage, we were told." Someone else said, "There isn't a breath of air today. Someone must have sneezed." The power was out for an hour. These brief outages tend to happen a lot whenever I am able to be at Crosswicks. Not only do all the lights go out, but the darkness is accompanied by an unusual silence. The TV and the CD player are suddenly quiet. The refrigerator stops humming. So does the pump for our water, which is powered by electricity. So, in winter, does the furnace. All the normal little ordinary sounds with which we are surrounded are stilled.

We always eat by candle or oil lamp light, but normally in the living room the lights are on, a CD is playing. There is something very different in the house when there is a power loss. Shadows move. With the ordinary background noise silenced we hear the creaking of the old boards and, quite often, the sound of a mouse in the walls, despite the presence of three cats who are fairly good about doing their duty to keep the house free of rodents. The dogs tend to want to come closer, to press up against one of us. There is something intimate about the dark, although I find myself hoping that when it is time for bed the power will be back on so that I can turn on my bed lamp and read. But we are less aware of all the manmade things with which we are surrounded when the power goes out, and more aware of the mystery of the universe.

After the automobile accident I was aware of many primitive fears, fear of the dark being one of them. For the first time that I can remember I slept with a night light, needing that comforting glow. When we got on the little ship to go to Antarctica I had expected to leave the bathroom door open a crack so that I would see some light. But on a ship a door is either open or closed. So, for the first time in nearly six months I slept in the dark.

In the summer of 1994 Luci Shaw and I took a ten-day trip together through the Canadian Rockies to celebrate her sixty-fifth and my seventy-fifth birthdays. We stayed in a couple of miserable hotels in order to afford being able to stay in a couple of excellent ones, and we were in a beautiful hotel near Lake Louise when there was a heavy thunderstorm and all the power in the area went out. Most of the hotels had enough subsidiary power for kitchens and dining rooms, but not for the other public rooms and certainly not for the guest bedrooms. We had a latish dinner and went to our rooms to go to bed; what else was there to do? And in the morning we both admitted to each other, shame-faced, that we had had difficulty getting to sleep because we could not read. We had each been given a candle in a bubbly glass holder, but its light was not nearly strong enough for us to be able to see the page of a book. How conditioned we are! Reading is part of our bedtime routine, of letting go the day and sliding into night and sleep.

Darkness is an Amma metaphor. When we snuggle up in bed at night in the dark, if we are able to go to bed safely, kindly, with a reasonable expectation of waking up to the challenges of a new day, the dark is similar to the darkness within the womb, where the unborn baby is warm and safe.

One of the current theories about our universe is that what is visible matter, to our eyes and to our telescopes, is only about half of the matter there is. Much of the matter in the universe is what is called dark matter, matter which we cannot see. That may well be true of us, too. The part of us which we can see, touch, feel, understand, is only the smallest part of us, and all our light matter is side by side with dark matter, and until the dark matter is acknowledged it can be destructive. We tend to want to sweep our dark matter under the bed, to pretend that it does not exist. But it is part of us, and must be acknowledged. Unlike the dark matter that is out in space, we can bring our own dark matter up into the light; it, too, was made by God. It, too, has a purpose, a loving purpose. Nothing needs to be hidden from a loving mother. All can be accepted, forgiven, redeemed.

And it may be that there are parts of us that grow best in the dark, that are sheltered and protected by the dark. We need our night times, when we can let go the business and busyness of the day, and relax in the shelter of the almighty wings. In one of our prayers for the dead we ask that "light perpetual shine upon them." That sounds to me like Chinese water torture. Rather than light perpetual I want to ask for uncreated light, that light which has nothing to do with daylight but has, instead, to do with the heart. We come across the words *uncreated light* in the works of many theologians, and because I live in the created order, as part of it, I am not sure what uncreated light is. It is that light which was before there was light, that light which was part of the Word which called created light into being. It is, mostly, a mystery, but a shining mystery.

In the words of one of our hymns, "In him there is no darkness at all, the night and the day are both alike. The lamb is the lamp of the city of God, shine in my heart, Lord Jesus!"

Uncreated light is probably as available at night as by day, in the dark as in light. It is a mystery which is outside the created universe, and the created universe itself is mysterious enough! No one, neither theologian nor scientist, knows why it is here at all. Why should there be anything? My friend Tallis said that God is love, and it is in the nature of love to create. That is as good an answer as any.

In the dark, even more than in the light, I am aware in a poignant way of those who have been with me in Crosswicks, that house which is well over two hundred fifty years old, aware of those before me and in my lifetime who have died. Tallis spent many weekends with us. On most of his visits he celebrated the Holy Mysteries. He married two of our children at Crosswicks. He shared much of the pain of my mother's dying, of my husband's. And of course Hugh is all through the house. It was our first—and only—house. It was there we learned to hang wallpaper, to paint woodwork, to dig in the garden, to can and freeze fruits and vegetables. There is not a room in the house that does not hold vivid memories of Hugh.

Houses have their own personalities. Several people, walking into Crosswicks, have remarked, "What a loving house!" It is. It is a loving and welcoming house. It promises comfort, not protection from the ordinary troubles of life, but comfort when we are sad, when we cry. It has a maternal quality as it surrounds each one of us with quiet love.

So the house itself is an icon. If it had to be *my* house it would no longer be an icon; it would be an idol.

We hear a lot about our shadows nowadays. We have come a long way from Robert Louis Stevenson's

> I have a little shadow who goes in and out with me,
> And what can be the use of him is more than I
>   can see.

But I think it is still difficult for some people to understand the reason for their shadow. Too many people see their shadow selves as the bad, the evil part of their personalities, but shadows are more probably like that dark matter which makes up half of the universe and has only fairly recently been recognized.

The twentieth-century physicists' discovery that most thrills me is that the universe is totally interrelated, light, dark, large, small, all are one, one universe, in which each part affects every other part. Indeed the movement of the stars does affect us. Conversely, it would seem that what we do affects the stars, and that's what knocks our socks off. Wild! We can't understand or accept the complexity of the universe, nor that what we do does make a difference.

We know that we use only a fragment of our complex and extraordinary brains. Perhaps our understanding of our place in creation lies in that untapped portion. Perhaps our understanding of our shadow selves also lies in that unused part of our grey matter. Some of what I do not understand about myself is undoubtedly part of my self I do not want to recognize, because I'd rather not face it. I probably wouldn't like it; I might even be ashamed of it. But some of it may be quite marvelous! A lot of the shadow self is the home of poetry, story, prayer. My deepest understandings are often released from the part of me of which I am least aware most of the time.

Mystics throughout the ages have been willing to go into the dark, knowing that the deeper they go the closer they are to the love which made all things. Artists of all disciplines must be willing to go into the dark, let go control, be surprised. It may be small wonder that both saints and artists often express their shadow selves in unacceptable ways because without this release the accumulated steam might make them blow up. And some of them indeed have blown up, have gone mad. This does not excuse or condone drunkenness or sexual license, but it explains some of it. If I have to accept that the brighter the light in a mortal, the darker the shadow, I also have to accept that the darker the shadow, the brighter the light.

What is my own shadow? If we all had the ability to recognize our shadows we might not be driven by them. I was an extraordinarily serious small child. Life around me was serious, in my home, with my father's constant coughing; in school, with insensitive and punitive teachers; in the world, where the nations were preparing for yet another war. It was not until my high school years, in Ashley Hall where I found encouragement and friendship, that I realized that I had to learn how to laugh.

Laughter did not come easily. I experimented with laughter, listening to my voice as I tried to make the right noises. It was a long time before laughter became spontaneous for me, and even longer before laughter became so delightful that I nearly fell off my chair with the joy of it. The seriousness that still sometimes causes my laughter to remain hidden may be part of my shadow. So is my insecurity, my fear of rejection, even though I have learned where some of these shadows come from. I do not think we know all of our shadows; perhaps they are revealed to us as we are able to bear them.

Did Jesus, the mortal Jesus, recognize his? Was the story of the blasted fig tree an acting out of that shadow? I do not think this is a blasphemous question. Jesus put on full mortality for our sakes, otherwise he is God only pretending to be human.

Maker of the stars, Maker of me, I do not understand, but I love you for your love of us, for all of us, for every sparrow, every galaxy, every gnat, every drop of water and all that is within it, universes within universes, and all made by you, with love.

Alleluia.

9

WORDS

Word
I, who live by words, am wordless when
I try my words in prayer. All language turns
To silence. Prayer will take my words and then
Reveal their emptiness. The stilled voice learns
To hold its peace, to listen with the heart
To silence that is joy, is adoration.
The self is shattered, all words torn apart
In this strange patterned time of
    contemplation
That, in time, breaks time, breaks words,
    breaks me,
And then, in silence, leaves me healed and
    mended.
I leave, returned to language, for I see
Through words, even when all words are
    ended.
I, who live by words, am wordless when
I turn me to the Word to pray. Amen.

Ultimately words are useless, and yet, penultimately, they are all we
have. And the Word has blessed our human words.

"In the beginning was the Word, and the Word was with God, and the Word was God."

Words have always had an iconic quality for me. But, as with all icons, I must be very careful not to turn words into idols.

"In the beginning was the Word," we affirm, and then we smugly smirch that word with our pride, our irreverence, with the arrogance of our minds.

How little we know ourselves! How desperately we need the part of ourselves which has been left in the dark.

How wonderful that we can put words together, and that they will mean something, tell a story, offer hope! But far too often we use language carelessly, stupidly, and we contradict ourselves and don't even know it. I'm an avid bumper sticker watcher, and it is chastening how often bumper stickers show how we manage to fool ourselves. Will Campbell told of seeing two bumper stickers on one car. One said, "U.S. Army. Be All that You Can Be." The other read, "Abortion Kills."

He used that not to get into an argument pro or con abortion, but as an example of how horrendously we can deceive and contradict ourselves without even realizing it.

We human beings are the creature who uses language. We put words together so that we can tell someone of our love, so that we can sing of that love in a song, write of it in a novel. We can also use words to destroy. The old adage "sticks and stones may break my bones but words will never hurt me" is simply not true. Words can and do hurt, stinging and scarring us. But words can also be icons. How can we contemplate, without trembling repentance, this troubled century which has known two terrible world wars, as well as countless ambiguous wars? How can we remember the concentration camps, and what was done to the Jews, Gypsies, homosexuals, dissidents, and others Hitler considered dangerous to his glorious Aryan society, without anguish? We cannot disassociate ourselves from it, nor from the current evils. Nor can we forget it, or try to convince other generations it didn't happen, as some people are presently trying to do. Our memories do distort past events, but we cannot wipe them out as though they had never happened!

In my city I cannot pull my skirts away and separate myself from the street people, the pimps, the drug pushers, the wounded and sick and angry people I see every day. Nor can I separate myself from those who in all centuries have held to the light, have snatched children from burning houses at risk of their own lives, have done their best to feed and clothe and share in the pain of those who are hungry in body, mind, and spirit. We are a rich mix, and while at times it seems that the wicked outweigh the good, it is foolish to play the numbers game. As long as there are even a few who are truly serving the light, as long as there is the remnant, we need not despair.

I have a friend, the leader of my house church, a woman, who in this dark world gives me great light. She and her family live a few blocks away from me, and so we often see the same panhandlers. She does not have money to spare, with four children to feed and educate and a scientist husband whose teaching salary has to be stretched to its limit. She herself has gone back to full-time teaching, now that the baby is walking and talking. But when a panhandler comes to her, she asks the person's name so that she can pray for whoever it is. She knows many of the local street people by name and worries if they are not in their usual stations. Because she is Black, as are a majority of the street people in our area, it may be easier for her to get close to them than it is for me, but she has taught me a great deal. Now when I offer food, I also ask for a name, and timidly (I need more courage) offer prayer. Her words have become icons for me.

Words of prayer are the opposite of words of condemnation, and yet I must pray for forgiveness for my own condemnation of those who condemn. Even in my praying for the condemners, I am still, in a way, condemning. It is not easy. At least prayer is a beginning, as long it is not coercive, as in "Lord, make these hard-hearted people repent! Convert them to *my* kind of Christianity!" More and more I am simply holding out myself, and those I love, and those I do not love, to a Maker whose love is beyond my comprehension but who is the core of my faith.

Words have a potency we seem to have forgotten. One of my friends, a woman in her late fifties, was suddenly struck down by an aneurysm, and when it had been decided that no "heroic" measures should be used, a priest friend stood by her bed in the hospital, told her how much she was loved, and then said, "Now, good Christian soul, depart," and she died.

Words have power. Sometimes we need permission to die.

Good Christian soul, depart.

U.S. Army: Be all that you can be. Abortion kills.

What radically opposite use of words.

We do not always know what we're saying; we do not always know what we're asking. But we can be more careful than we are.

One thing we can do is check out the buzz words as they come along, to see if they're helping us hide from something we'd rather not know about, close our eyes to something we'd rather not see, protect ourselves from pain we'd rather not experience.

It horrifies me how phallic the language of nuclear warfare is. One of my granddaughters gave me an article on this language which she was reading for a class. It was pretty blatant. There was a need to "harden our missiles"; there was talk about "vertical erector launchers." There was "penetration" and "deep thrust." When India detonated her first nuclear weapon it was referred to as "losing her virginity." Big little boys playing terrible games. "Nuke speak" is one of our uglier jargons.

Then there is "politically correct."

Not long ago I was asked to preach at a Black church in Harlem, in New York City. I was deeply honoured at this request, and I worked hard on my sermon and was graciously and warmly received. A week or so later someone asked me what I had preached about. I replied, "Jonah, and God's forgiveness."

I was told, "That was politically very incorrect."

For a moment I was too startled to speak. Then I said, "Well, since I follow a man who was so totally politically incorrect that he was crucified for it, I guess I'll take that as a compliment."

I'm not even sure what being politically correct means. I think we're supposed to espouse the right causes. As I've written elsewhere, being involved with a "cause" helps us not to come into too close contact with the people who make up the cause. Jesus was not interested in the cause of women, or lepers, or Samaritans. He cared about the people. He showed compassion in his words and in his actions. The protagonists of his stories are women, or lepers, or Samaritans, the untouchables of his day. One can be impeccably politically correct and remain hard of heart, rigid, and judgmental. Political correctness may have value, as long as it is not used as a shield against the reality of human problems.

Dysfunctional. God help us, sometimes those labeled dysfunctional function better than the rest of us. A young friend of mine who has been through a nasty divorce, not of her own choosing, who is raising her kids the best she can, says she hates the label. So she should. Under the most difficult circumstances she is functioning extremely well.

I have known people who have looked back on their not unusual childhoods and have done their best to label them dysfunctional because that's popular right now; it's the "in" thing and can be used as an excuse for all kinds of problems. "Well, I can't help it; it's not my fault, you know. I come from a dysfunctional family." The people I know best who have come from brutally dysfunctional families do not make much of their ugly past, but get along as well as they can in the present. I suspect my childhood family might readily be labeled dysfunctional, but I learned so much from it I wouldn't want anything changed—except maybe some of my middle-grade teachers.

Jargon is seldom helpful and usually gives us excuses not to think about what the jargon word really means.

Meanwhile writers are still struggling with language, trying to find the right word—the word which clarifies and illumines. Theological committees tend to underestimate the capacity of the ordinary lay person. When I asked why, in the Prayer Book General Thanksgiving, God's *inestimable love* had been changed to *immeasurable love*, I was told that the laity found *inestimable* difficult. That's pretty condescending, in the nastiest sense of that word. *Immeasurable* is not simpler than *inestimable*, and in the context of that glorious prayer of Thanksgiving it is a weaker word. When I asked a multi-PhD-ed clergyman why *the quick and the dead* had been changed to *the living and the dead*, I was told that young people did not know the word, *quick*. I asked, "How are they going to know it if you take it away from them?"

Quick is a good word. For a pregnant woman, a glorious moment is when the baby first quickens, when she can feel the tender movement of the child in the womb. Quickening is a marvelous affirmation of the reality of the life within. When you cut your nail below the quick, you know it. It's a living, bleeding word, and another example of the underestimation of the ordinary person in the pew. Substituting words because a group of academic people have decided they are easier for the ignorant public is another kind of golden calf.

Of course I am not suggesting that language should not grow, shift, change. A living language is constantly changing. What I am objecting to is the manipulation of language by the academic elite because they underestimate the ordinary, faithful churchgoers.

Scientists can be just as obfuscating as theologians. The magazine of *Chemical and Engineering News* (to which I do not subscribe, but my daughter-in-law's chemist father does) gave me this: "Lamda is a cosmological natural constant from Einstein's equations, which, until recently, was defined as zero due to its negligible numerical value." And, to give us another smile, on the same page was printed, taken from what was called "a respected weekly magazine," this: "[The author] neither accidentally nor intentionally omits or includes anything that could support a preconceived thesis."

Imagination, however, is often visible in the world of particle physics, although Dr. Anne Eisenberg, a professor at Polytechnic University in Brooklyn, says scientists think that "there's something suspect about it if you make it understandable." This is from an article in *The New York Times* which continues, "There's tremendous snobbery against the comprehensible . . . . The bad side of that is the snobbery. The good side of that is that it reflects the desire for scientific precision."

I wonder if it's only snobbery, or if it doesn't reflect the child's delight in a secret language, known only to a few special pals, while the rest of the kids are on the outside and can't understand?

The *Times* article continues to tell us that Dr. James A. Yorke (who gave us the word *chaos* "to describe the mathematical behaviour of dynamical physical systems like flowing water or weather, which cannot be predicted in the long term") says that "Words empower us to think about other things, and we must think of the words that allow us to do that." Not bad advice for a writer of stories, either.

Words are icons when they are open doors, when they lead us beyond ourselves over new horizons. But they can also make us want to stay in closed systems, where any change is considered heresy. Words can indeed be either icons or idols.

So let me not make my passion for words into a golden calf, either, or I may fail to recognize the wonder of language changing as it emerges out of the experience of living in these last years of a troubled century.

There are many words which have wonderful connotations: love, children, joy, play, sunlight, daffodils, spring, autumn leaves, trees, truth, friends, grandchildren, books, stories, truth, freedom, compassion, responsibility, caring, healing—these are just a few words off the top of my head.

Some words have connotations that at one time are good, at one time are negative; for instance, integrity, which is now too often a pop word for self-indulgence. The negative words that bother me most are the popular words that make us feel *au courant*, so that we do not have to think about what they really mean: fundamentalist, for instance!

Not only are we asked to be politically correct, but environmentally correct. Both kinds of correctness keep us from considering seriously what we should be thinking or doing either politically or environmentally.

I have written about my abhorrence of the word *consumer*. And I much prefer *love* or *friendship* to *relationship*. I also believe we need a word between *acquaintance* and *friend*.

Without words we cannot tell stories. We can hug and kiss, but we cannot say, "I love you."

We can look at the glory of the sunrise or the brilliance of the stars, but without words we cannot ask, "Who made you?" We cannot say, "Maker of the universe and of me, I trust you." We can feel hunger or lust or fatigue, but we cannot ask questions.

How aware are we that many words that used to be considered common are no longer in our vocabulary? How aware are we that we are being manipulated by the media to accept a smaller vocabulary, one that will make us less able to resist their demands that we buy, buy, buy—and become consumers?

Recently I came across a wonderful line of Tom Stoppard's: "The media—it sounds like a convention of spiritualists."

Some of the old words still have vital, current meaning. Some do not. Language changes. If it does not change, like Latin it dies. But we need to be aware that as our language changes, so does our theology change, particularly if we are trying to manipulate language for a specific purpose. That is what is happening with our attempts at inclusive language, which thus far have been inconclusive and unsuccessful.

Certainly the old, patriarchal language, which often appears to hate women as well as to exclude them (i.e., woman as the whore of Babylon), needs changing. But not with a chip on the shoulder, not from a need for the female to dominate rather than the male. In language, as in life, male and female need to love each other, participate in each other, not control, not wield power. Perhaps our theology does need changing, but we must be careful not to change it inadvertently, without realizing or understanding what we are doing. Theology, our language about God, develops slowly but definitely throughout Scripture, from the tribal god to the loving, Abba God shown us by Jesus. Do we want a less loving God today as we struggle to bring the feminine back into the language? Should not the feminine mean love, tenderness, mystery, hope? Mostly it doesn't, not right now, and so for many of us the attempts at inclusive language have not worked. We need more poets, more artists who understand how to express in metaphor and icon that which cannot be expressed in finite words.

Jesus. Christ. Here are words which should be totally iconic, but are, far too often, idolatrous. When I am asked, "Are you a Christian?" If I answer, Yes, my questioner may either lay on my shoulders all the horrors done in the name of Christ, or discount me because I am not Christian in exactly the approved way.

After the Holocaust, I thought that Christians could never again treat another race, another religion, with brutality that sought to wipe out, destroy, with genocide. Despite the pervasive presence of the media, we do not truly know what is going on in Bosnia, but what we do know causes anguish—not only to us, but to God, to Christ. The slaughter in Rwanda of the Tutsis by the Hutus—and vice versa—is equally horrifying.

One Sunday afternoon, driving home from a job, we turned on the car radio to "All Things Considered," and came in on an interview with the most popular Rwandan singer. He talked a great deal about the need for reconciliation in Rwanda, and the interviewer asked him if he, himself, had been touched by the slaughter. He replied, in a quiet voice, that his mother and father, his sister, his little brothers, had all been shot and killed.

He was asked, then, how he could talk as he did about reconciliation.

His answer was that to respond to violence with violence serves no good purpose. Reconciliation was the only hope.

There was no indication on the program about the religious faith, if any, of this man. But he, to me, exemplified what I hope for in Christianity. Indeed, he is one of the saints.

And all across the planet war continues. Is this new genocide for the sake of religion or for the sake of land? As we make our way through Scripture, it seems that a desire, a warring desire, to have someone else's land is expressed in almost every chapter.

Because of the enormity of the universe which is vast beyond the powers of my imagination, I need the Incarnation, I need Jesus, the God I can see, hear, feel. But I do not ever want to use Christ as a weapon. What kind of evangelism is that? Shouldn't my love of Christ be a light that is visible? Shouldn't it be a lovingness in me that prohibits me from wanting to dominate anyone else? I want to share, not dominate.

And that's another interesting word, leading my thinking to others: dominate—dominance—dominant—domineering—dominie—domina—domicile. Do they all come from the same root? According to my etymological dictionary, they do. However, a Scottish dominie was more like a shepherd than an omnipotent ruler. The shepherd leads, rather than dominates, no matter how stupid the sheep!

Imagination is a word that is currently suspected by the fundalits as being dangerous. Often in Scripture we read the phrase "the imagination of their hearts"; in context it seems to mean willfulness, self-will, rather than the glory of our imaginations which permit us to affirm the Incarnation!

Words do change. We no longer think of *prevent* as meaning "go before," which is it's real meaning: *pre venire*—go before, lead, guide.

Another change in words which shows a change in thinking is shown in the way young women no longer call their monthly periods "the curse," as it was known when I was young. My friend Luci Shaw grew up with the phrase, "being unwell," from her mother's Victorian generation. I have sometimes called menstruation the "time of the moon," which I rather like. Most young women nowadays simply say that they have their period.

When I went to an American boarding school after having been in an English one, I asked why one of the girls wasn't in class. I was told, "Oh, she isn't feeling very well. She fell off the roof."

"Is she badly hurt?" I asked in horror.

And was told that that was yet another phrase for the monthly period.

It is strange that our language about God has not changed noticeably with the radical changes that have come with our understanding of quantum mechanics, or the theory of chaos, or the mysteries of particle physics. Shouldn't our awareness of the magnificence of the universe change our language about our Maker? There are more galaxies than our most sophisticated instruments can count. It is quite possible that there is more than one "universe"; there may be many. It takes all the imagination of my heart to pray to a Maker who has made more than I can comprehend, but who is also able to care for each one of us with individual love. Theologians talk about a God who is both immanent and transcendent, but God still seems to many Christians to be the God of this one small planet, and only the Christian part of the planet, at that.

It is easier to be a fundalit than to think, to affirm, to use our God-given imaginations. Fundalitism, taken to its extreme, leads to rigidity and to the development of sects where the leader dominates rather than leads. A current very black joke about the Branch Davidians is that in their violent demise they wanted to keep up with the Joneses. It's an *ugly* joke, but then the brutality of such sects is equally ugly.

Walter Wink points out that it is ironic indeed that many literalists see Jesus in the Second Coming doing everything that he steadfastly refused to do during his lifetime. "Teeth will be provided," indeed!

If we take every word in Scripture literally we do not have to use our imaginations, and I suspect we cannot possibly read all of Scripture, some of which is pretty wild (I am particularly fond of those dry bones in Ezekiel coming back to life). And when I am feeling hard of heart or judgmental, I reread Jonah, with its affirmation of God's forgiving love. One young man told me earnestly that when the great fish regurgitated Jonah out on the shore, he was bleached white because of the gastric juices in which he had sat. A fish large enough to swallow even a small prophet would have gastric juices strong enough to digest him! Why can't we see the story of Jonah as a true story about our slowness to forgive, our eagerness to condemn, and God's *inestimable* love and forgiveness?

I have previously quoted Karl Barth, "I take the Bible far too seriously to take it literally," but it is only just now with this discussion of Jonah that I have realized that if we take the Bible literally we don't have to take it seriously.

I need to remember that with compassion and not get so irritated by buzz words that I turn them into a reverse sort of golden calf.

"Inclusive language" is another buzz word, but I've talked about it elsewhere. Some of our language is grossly insensitive. It will change as we change, as our love of God grows and we learn to honour all life on this planet. It is a small planet indeed, and we no longer have room for *us* and *them,* as our various terrible ethnic wars are showing us. We are more like the Hutus and the Tutsis than we realize. We have a lot to learn before we can understand that all of us are indeed brothers and sisters and that we have to live together, with all our differences. (Theodore Sturgeon wrote a story called "If All Men Were Brothers Would You Want Your Sister to Marry One?") I am looking forward to the time when we can tell ethnic jokes not disparagingly but because we love each other and treasure each other's idiosyncrasies, and we can laugh joyously together. Will that happen before the heavenly banquet? Perhaps it has to happen here on earth before we'll be ready for the heavenly banquet.

My friend Luci Shaw and I are working hard to put together a book about friendship, and we don't want to write just another book about friendship at this time in our culture where friendship is another trampled word. It is also a deeply iconic word for me, and indeed, writing this book together has enlarged and deepened the friendship. Emerson wrote: "Give me friendships, for I am weary of the superficial."

When friendships become superficial, misunderstanding develops and feeds on itself. The war between men and women is worse than I've ever known it to be, and I'm not sure why. It's always been bad, from the time we lived in caves and trees, but it seems to be accelerating in this last decade of our deeply troubled century. Perhaps the suspicion men and women have about each other is a mask for our fear and hatred of ourselves, us mortals. We human creatures too often don't like people. We don't trust people. We call people human beings because we're afraid of the word *mortal*. We don't want to acknowledge that we are mortal. But we are. We are born, and we will die.

So we're reluctant to use the word *mortal* because it's a scary word. We don't like it. It terrifies us, no matter how deeply Christian we are. We make up heavens and hells that are idolatrous. The traditional fundalit heaven sounds totally dull, and I don't believe God is ever dull. The traditional fundalit hell sounds more interesting simply because all the most interesting people will be there.

Is it because we are mortal that we don't dare leave our immortality to God?

We blunt our awareness by substituting buzz words for a deeper vocabulary.

We substitute:

human being	for mortal
memorial service	for funeral
relationship	for love and friendship
passing away	for dying
long illness	for cancer or AIDS
entitlement	for heritage
Holy Spirit	for Holy Ghost
the Spirit	for Holy Spirit
and also with you	for and with your spirit
sanitation engineer	for garbage collector
custodian	for janitor
administrative assistant	for secretary
mentally challenged	for retarded
chronologically advantaged (or disadvantaged)	for old
senior citizen	for elderly person

I am seventy-seven. I am old, and I enjoy my years and all that experience has given me. Doesn't wisdom matter anymore? I was a bright child at five, but wisdom takes time. Years. I'm not there yet. But I'm working at it.

Are we assuming that there is work which is beneath us? That if we admit we try to keep a city clean and disease-free by removing the garbage we are not significant? Have the affluent among us made the garbage collector feel so insignificant that a euphemism has to replace the strong and vigorous reality? When I was a little girl growing up in the great city of New York, there were men called White Wings. They wore white pants and tops, and they wheeled white canvas barrels, and they had long sticks with metal points which helped them pick up the debris of the city and keep New York clean. In this filthy city, why don't we employ White Wings again? Is cleaning the city more demeaning than picking up a welfare check? Wouldn't those—and there should be women as well as men—who kept the streets clean have a sense of work well done, of pride, that might lead them to spend their money on food and rent and maybe a good book rather then drugs? It's a useless question because I think the return of the White Wings is unlikely, and that is part of the sickness of the city—and not the city only.

I spent a night in a Seattle hotel, and the next morning, reading the paper over breakfast, I came across these linguistic substitutions:

divorce	marriage dissolution
divorce attorneys	family law practitioners
alimony	spousal maintenance
custody	residential parent

In order to avoid wholeness and holiness we substitute easy words for tough ones, or cumbersome words for simple ones. In the olden days philosophers and theologians used to have a skull on their desks so that they would not forget to contemplate their mortality. We nowadays avoid such thoughts at all costs, another reason I am grateful for the translators who say "mortal" rather than "human being."

Dust we are and to dust we shall return, but our mortal lives are forever dignified because God Almighty became one of us.

Someone told of a child who asked, "Why did Jesus have to die?" and said that this was *the* important question. To me the more important one is "Why was Jesus born?" Since he was born, he was going to have to die. Mortals die. But why did the immortal one have to become mortal? Can we even begin to understand or accept such love?

Our understanding comes in glimpses, and through icons. The two character assassins who wrote the book against me accuse me of worshipping Buddha. No. I don't. In *A Circle of Quiet* I tell of the white china laughing Buddha which sits on my desk at Crosswicks. If I worshipped that small piece of china surely it would be an idol and the accusation might have some validity. But I don't. I love it because the smile of compassion, tolerance, joy, helps put me back into proportion. I can look at a crucifix and feel sorry for myself, but I cannot look at the look of ineffable radiance on that white china face and feel self-pity. This white china Buddha is an icon, a Christ figure for me. Another help I am given when I look at that smile is a sorrow for my judgmentalism, and at least a hope of more compassion and understanding of those whose view of Christ and the universe is so totally different from mine that I am seen as a threat. If I respond by feeling threatened (and sometimes I do), I am falling into the same trap as the accusers. Can I make a judgment without being judgmental? Jesus did. I ought to be able to, also. Sometimes I can, and that is a blessing.

I who live by words am still struggling to turn me to the Word in prayer.

10

TRINITY

"We worship one God in Trinity, and the Trinity in Unity," reads the Athanasian Creed, which continues,

There is one Person of the Father, another of
    the Son, and another of the Holy Ghost.
But the Godhead of the Father, of the Son, and
    of the Holy Ghost, is all one. . . .
Such as the Father is, such is the Son, and
    such is the Holy Ghost.
The Father uncreate, the Son uncreate, and
    the Holy Ghost uncreate. . . .
The Father incomprehensible, the Son
      incomprehensible, and the Holy Ghost
      incomprehensible.
The Father eternal, the Son eternal, and the
    Holy Ghost eternal.
And yet they are not three eternals, but one
    eternal.
As also there are not three uncomprehensibles,
    nor three uncreated, but one uncreated,
    and one incomprehensible.

Dorothy Sayers adds, "the whole thing incomprehensible," to which I add, "Thank God!"

If it were comprehensible, nobody would have struggled to make it comprehensible in the various creeds of the church(es). Nobody has yet succeeded, and perhaps the very incomprehensibility is why we no longer pay more than lip service to Trinity Sunday, but slide over it and immediately forget it.

When Hugh and I worshipped in the small Congregational Church in our village, it was not a liturgical church and we didn't pay any attention to Trinity Sunday. We paid attention to Christmas and Easter, but that was all. We didn't observe Lent, or Epiphany, of Advent, or any of the other great seasons of the church year. Now that our Congregational church has joined the United Church of Christ, this has changed, and we mark the seasons and this, to me, gives an added richness to our observance.

But now Trinity Sunday in even the most liturgical of churches is paid little heed. The Trinity is a wholeness which has become too difficult for us to understand. It's never been easy, but at least we used to declare our belief in the Trinity as intrinsic to Christianity. Now we have the great feast of Pentecost, and Trinity Sunday comes and goes and after that we're into the long series of Sundays after Pentecost, replacing what I used to think of as the long green Sundays after Trinity.

The Trinity proclaims a unity that in this fragmented world we desperately need. We are mortals who are male and female, and we need to know each other, love each other. The world gets daily more perilous. Our cities spawn crime. Terrorists are around every corner. Random acts of violence increase.

Less understandable and less advertised is the sad fact that Christians are suspicious of other Christians. Are Roman Catholics Christian or aren't they? Why did Protestants and Catholics throughout the centuries each put down the other as being not Christian? Don't we have all the central things—God, making; Christ, awaking; the Holy Spirit, blessing—in common?

Do we have anybody to follow who is trustworthy? Where are our prophets? Surely not the televangelists or the gurus of the various "Christian" sects. If I affirm I have more in common with the people who throw rocks at me than I do with the New Agers or the Branch Davidians (or their equivalent), I am not always understood. Isn't love of God and joy in Christ and comfort in the Holy Spirit enough to hold us together? It seems not.

The Trinity was never meant to be comprehensible in the way that a mathematical formula is comprehensible. The writers of the Apostles' and the Nicene creeds affirmed that. Another thing we must remember about the Trinity is that it was always there, an icon of all three Persons, whole, undivided. The hardest Person of the Trinity to comprehend is Christ, because we must let go all our rational preconceptions and move into the mystery of love.

The great Arian controversy came from the difficulty of understanding the Trinity. Arius believed that there was a time when the son was not. Athanasius, in a white flame of outrage, affirmed that Christ always was. Perhaps some of the confusion came and comes from the fact that it is almost impossible for us to believe in the great action of love by the Word, the Second Person, in coming to us as Jesus. Christ always was, is, and will be. Jesus was born and died. Christ, as Jesus, came into time for us, into the microscopic seed in Mary's womb. It is beyond human comprehension, but not beyond human faith. Faith indeed is for what we cannot comprehend. Our finite minds are inadequate for the wonder of the Maker.

If all the Persons of the Trinity were always there, from the beginning, from before the beginning, then the argument over the "filioque clause" falls into ashes. In the Western Church we talk about the Spirit "Who proceeds from the Father and the Son." In the East the Spirit proceeded only from the Father. But if the Trinity is truly the Trinity, if every person of the Trinity was already and always there, then nobody proceeded from anybody, and I really don't see what the shouting is all about. Sometimes I wonder if it isn't simply an example of our need to argue. (A Sunday school teacher asked, "Who are the pagans?" A child replied, "The pagans are the people who don't quarrel about God.")

One explanation of the need for the doctrine of the Trinity is that it came into the Church in an attempt to explain Jesus, the Son of God. But this creates a problem because Jesus, the one born in Bethlehem in accordance with the prophets, was really not part of the Trinity at all, or, at best, was only a tiny exclamation point on the edge of the Trinity. This misunderstanding, that Jesus, the human man (also God!) who walked the earth for thirty-three years, was a full third of the Trinity, has caused some people to think of Jesus' last name as Christ. A common swearword I've encountered in numerous works of fiction comes when a character in stress or anger cries out "Jesus H. Christ!" I have no idea what the H. stands for. But Jesus Christ is not a name like Abraham Lincoln or Johann Sebastian Bach. The Second Person of the Trinity is Christ, Christ who was willing to leave heaven and, for a few years, very few in God's vast span of time, take on the mortality of Jesus of Nazareth, Jesus who was fully human as well as fully divine. That's the glorious impossibility of the Incarnation. Many people called this Jesus the Son of God. Jesus, very pointedly, always referred to himself as the Son of Man. As much as the limitations he had willingly taken on allowed, he understood himself to be the Called, the Chosen One. Even though he did not call himself the Son of God he referred frequently to his heavenly Father and the fact that they were, in an extraordinary, incomprehensible way, One.

If Jesus was an exclamation point on the edge of the Trinity, what an exclamation point he was! An alleluia of an exclamation point! An exclamation point that gives us Christianity. During his lifetime Jesus was misunderstood, so misunderstood that he was crucified. And then, to the surprise and awe and even terror of many, came the Resurrection, another exclamation point that turned the world upside down. We do well to remember something we seem to have forgotten, that Trinity Sunday is the fulfillment of the great festivals of Easter: Resurrection, Ascension, Pentecost, Trinity!

Alleluia!

There were many people who wanted him to be a political Messiah, a deliverer come to free the Jews from the domination of Rome, and these people refused to understand what his claim really was and that it was far greater than any claim to earthly power. But it is a claim that is beyond our mortal powers to prove, to explain, to understand, to comprehend. We can be irradiated by its glory. We can believe in it with joy. But none of the creeds or statements of faith explain it, no matter how hard the human writers try.

It was not difficult to misunderstand Jesus (we all do, to some extent), because what he was and what he said was part of the *Mysterium tremendum et fascinans,* a mystery so great, so fascinating, that theologians and philosophers and scholars have written and argued about it for two thousand years. But because mystery is essentially beyond proof, nothing has, in terms of literal fact, been proven. How can you prove such an act of love on the part of the most holy Trinity?

Of course, the Trinity, like any other concept about God, is no more than that, a concept, inadequate; a groping attempt to explain wholeness to a fragmented race of mortals. It is also an attempt to explain Jesus' state of being both wholly human and wholly divine. His human-ness came from his earthly mother, and his divinity from his heavenly Father.

The Trinity is an icon for us, to help us see God's love, and God's calling of each of us into completeness.

We do not understand our own wholeness. We are beginning to realize how our minds and our bodies interact, but as always, we go too far; we get out of balance. We slide back into the heresy that the body is evil, or on into the equally distorted materialistic heresy that the flesh is all there is. Or we put too much weight on the psyche, and tend to blame any ill of the body on anger, or stress, or jealousy. These emotions may lower the body's resistance to the common cold, may make anyone with a cold feel worse than when the mind is at peace, but they do not cause the cold. I was outraged when, after Hugh's death, someone asked me what he had been so angry about that it caused him to have cancer. I replied that we live on a polluted planet, and that more and more people are going to have cancer. I suspect that my questioner felt that if the cancer was somehow Hugh's fault, then it wouldn't be catching for the more virtuous.

There are some people who would like to have had my accident be caused by some flaw in me, but I was not driving the car in which I sat when a truck driver ran through a red light. Or, perhaps, they say, it was a punishment from God, for all my wrongdoings. No! Certainly I am encumbered by many wrongdoings, but a God of love does not punish in that way. Actions have consequences, and I suffered from the consequences of a truck driver's carelessness. A hemophiliac with AIDS is suffering from the consequences of unhealthy blood. Farmers whose crops have been ruined by floods are suffering the consequences of weather which, despite all our technology, is still unpredictable. None of these are punishments from God, but are consequences suffered in a universe where mortals have been given the extraordinary and terrifying gift of free will.

We have not yet recovered from the unscriptural idea that God is a God of anger, out to get us. I believe there is an enormous component of fear in Christians whose lives are spent in attacking other Christians. The unspoken rationale is that if we can blame someone else, we do not have to blame ourselves, and we therefore feel that we have inoculated ourselves against whatever problem the others have. In this fear there is a suspicion that we have to *earn* God's love. But God's love and forgiveness are given us by grace, as Scripture makes clear, perhaps particularly in the story of the landowner who paid all his workers the same wage, no matter how long or how short a time they had worked.

God: the whole Trinity, Father, Son, and Holy Spirit. Equal. The Judeo-Christian tradition is definitely patriarchal, and so is the Bible. But our religion was never meant to be static. We watch it move and grow from Genesis to Revelation, and we weren't meant to stop there and never change our attitude about or our understanding of God. Jesus called us to openness, wholeness, acceptance of mystery. He himself moved and changed, as I believe is shown in the story of the Syro-Phoenician woman who rebutted Jesus by saying that the dogs eat the crumbs from the children's table, and thereby opened the human Jesus to the extraordinary new thought that his mission was not only to the Jews, but to the entire world.

God the Father. How sad it is that many people's image of father is fierce and unloving, is of a bearded Victorian who is unapproachable and who loves to mete out punishments. I think of Elizabeth Barrett Browning's father, Moulton Barrett, who forced her to drink a glass of stout every night, much as she hated it. For her own good, he said. Was it? Or was it to show his own power? And isn't he the kind of image many people have of the Father?

My image of the Father, if I have to have one, is maternal, is, in fact, George MacDonald, so, yes, there is a beard, but there is also deep maternal love. It does not bother me that maternal is a feminine word, and George MacDonald was a male. When I call out to God in trouble or joy, as I often do, I think I am calling out to the whole Trinity, which is as far beyond our sexisms as love is beyond pornography.

God the Son. The Son, to most of us, is Jesus. But the Second Person of the Trinity is Christ, who was, before the worlds began, who is now, who always will be. Jesus is Christ who came briefly into time and then went back to the Godhead in a way we will never understand.

When I was struggling to be a "better" Christian, it was bad teaching about the Second Person of the Trinity that held me back. Pastors and other people tried to explain the unexplainable, make possible the impossible, put All Love in a test tube and say, Here!

No! The Incarnation can be understood only with the heart, not with the head. Literalism turns Christ-in-Jesus into imbalance. Only my heart can understand that Jesus was wholly God and wholly human.

In the greatest showing of love imaginable, Christ came into human life, into the story that love had made, as Jesus of Nazareth. Christ, the Second Person of the Trinity, left the place of Creation and power and became mortal, open to temptation, to weakness and fatigue, to sorrow and joy, and laughter and tears. Who was this Jesus? God? Mortal? Both? Yes, both! How could such a thing be?

It is impossible, but Jesus reiterated that although many things are impossible for us, nothing is impossible for God.

Even human love is beyond explanation. I am grateful for my life with my husband; grateful for my children (who are miracles in themselves), and for their children; grateful for the friends who accept me as I am, with all my faults and flaws, doubts, and mistakes.

I struggle to write about God and God's love, knowing that I am totally inadequate, and yet feeling called to proclaim a love so marvelous that it can only be wondered at and rejoiced in with delight.

I don't intellectually understand the Incarnation, but I know that it honours each one of our lives. We are all unique, all beloved, even those who seem to have been treated most unfairly by life, babies born with diseases that prevent them from growing either mentally or physically, infants addicted to drugs before they can talk, children beset by poverty, squalor, filth, abuse. Alas, we are not all equal; there is no equity; there is only love, love for every single one of us, no matter what life has done to us, or how we may have fouled or forfeited our own chances in life.

When I ask where Jesus would be in the upper west side of New York where I live, I know that he would be with the druggies, with the fourteen-year-old girls pushing their babies in flimsy strollers, many of them pregnant again; Jesus would be with those struggling against almost impossible odds to live a decent life despite all that is around them. He was with the poor and downtrodden because nobody else was. He was with those who were lepers or blind or possessed because nobody else was. They were devalued as human beings, and Jesus' presence affirmed their value. But he was also with Joseph of Arimathea and Nicodemus, and he wanted the rich young man as a disciple. He was with Martha and Mary and Lazarus of Bethany. And I think Jesus would also be with me and my friends, struggling in our own ways, carrying our own particular burdens, our own crosses.

It is sentimental to think that Jesus himself was one of the very poor, from a Judean barrio. Joseph was a carpenter, and so was Jesus, and carpenters were good, solid, middle-class citizens who worked hard and made a modest living, but were certainly not among the starving. Jesus had friends among the rich and among the middle class and among the poor.

And Christ, the Second Person of the Trinity, is not limited by the mortal body of Jesus of Nazareth. Christ is the Word who shouted all things into being and who continually calls each one of us into fuller being, every day, every minute, right now.

God the Holy Spirit, the Third Person of the Trinity, is for many people the most difficult aspect of all, but I suspect that for most artists the Holy Spirit is the easiest, for we know that whenever we do anything well we do not do it alone. We may call it inspiration, or even credit it to our own talent, but if we are honest we know that when we sing, write, paint, whatever is excitingly good transcends us. It is always awesome to think: Did I do that? Was I actually used to produce that painting, that poem? Play that sonata?

Musical instruments are icons of the Holy Spirit. My piano must be kept in tune. A violin or cello must equally be lovingly cared for, or when the moment of wonder comes the instrument will not be fit to receive it and turn it into music.

So we, ourselves, are instruments, vessels of the Holy Spirit, and therefore to be honoured and cared for so that when the Holy One wants to use us, we will be usable, in tune. We are not, always, more's the tragedy. But we can try.

And is the Holy Spirit he or she? I couldn't care less. The Holy Spirit is the Holy Spirit. Why do we try to diminish the glory with sexuality? It's like asking if energy is male or female. Perhaps those who call the rain female, rocks male, the night female, mountains male, are less hung up on sexuality than we are who call the ocean *it*.

The Holy Trinity, complete, always there, creating, loving, blessing, being with us in the fullness of love. In Roland Bainton's *The Church of Our Fathers* he shows a triangular diagram, with Father and Son at the top corners, the Holy Spirit at the bottom. The lines of the triangle are joined in such a way that they read, "The Father is not the Son or the Holy Spirit, the Son is not the Father or the Holy Spirit, the Holy Spirit is not the Father or the Son." They also read, "The Father is God, the Son is God, the Holy Spirit is God." It makes a certain amount of paradoxical sense. It is also another proof that the Trinity cannot be clearly diagramed or proven. Any diagram is merely another icon to open our eyes to a God who is beyond all our explanations.

The Trinity is limitless and we mortals want limits, limits to what is demanded of us, limits to God's love, limits to those God is willing to redeem, limits to those who are going to be saved. Redemption is Trinitarian, and it is not just for us human creatures; it is for all of Creation, angels and archangels, principalities and powers, thrones, cherubim and seraphim, stars, galaxies, mitochondria, all that has been made. We will truly understand the Trinity only when there is total reconciliation, the terrible and total reconciliation Irish poet James Stephens shows us in this poem, called "In the Fullness of Time":

> On a rusty iron throne
> In the farthest bounds of space,
> I saw Satan sit alone.
> Old and haggard was his face,
> For his work was done and he
> Rested in eternity.
>
> Down to him from out the sun
> Came his brother and his friend
> Saying, "Now the work is done,
> Enmity is at an end."
> And he guided Satan to
> Paradise that he knew.
>
> Uriel, without a frown,
> Michael without a spear,
> Gabriel came winging down,
> Welcoming their ancient peer,
> And they seated him beside
> One who had been crucified.

This extraordinary poem was sent to me by a friend after a conference during which we had spent some time in thinking about God's infinite forgiveness and our finite rebellion and hardness of heart. When I read those last two lines tears rushed to my eyes. I called a friend who was struggling with anger and incomprehension at the vicissitudes and injustices of life and read it to her, and she was horrified. She had been brought up a fundalit, taught about God's eternal displeasure with those who were destined to burn forever in hell. I do not think that it was in her loving heart to affirm eternal damnation, but early learning is hard to displace. I am forever grateful that my early learning was of a loving and forgiving God, a God who longs for us all to return to Love, mortals, angels, yes, and fallen angels, and even the most fallen angel of all.

Someone asked me, "Would you be willing to sit down at the table with those women who wrote that book about you?"

Yes, I would, though being together at the same table might be more difficult for them than for me. I do pray for reconciliation between us, without either wanting to control or manipulate the other. Reconciliation is part of my understanding of Trinity. In my little travel icon those three angels are angels of reconciliation in a world of pain and injustice and bitter anger. They call for us to sit by Abraham's tent and have a meal together, understanding all that that implies.

In the Night Prayers in the New Zealand Prayer Book the three persons of the Trinity are referred to as Earth Maker, Pain Bearer, Life Giver, and that is illuminating for me.

At the time of the peace treaty between Jew and Arab much was made of the shaking of hands by Rabin and Arafat. The newscasters skipped over the fact that the two leaders had been invited to have dinner together with the Clintons at the White House, and they refused. What matters in the Middle East is eating together. You cannot kill someone you have shared a meal with. And so my heart sank. When will they eat together?

When will we all eat together, God's children of all colours, all ways of worship? When will we be one in the kingdom, sharing in the unity of the Trinity?

II

THE BIBLE

The Bible: One of our greatest icons, and one of our greatest golden calves. The greater an icon is, the more dangerously easy it is for us to turn it into an idol.

Remember: an icon is never a thing of worship in itself. When the Bible becomes a thing in itself, rather than the word of God, it becomes an idol. How many of us understand the divine language? We are like small children struggling to learn to talk, making mistakes, often funny ones, as we try out words, hoping that what we say will be what we mean.

I try to read the Bible with an open heart and with as few preconceptions as possible. I try not to impose the thought patterns of the late twentieth century on the way people thought three and four and five thousand years ago. The deepest messages of the Bible are universal, but the dietary laws, for instance, are not particularly useful for our day. It was unwise to eat pork when trichinosis abounded, to eat shellfish when sea waters were unclean and disease ridden. Some of the advice for farmers is excellent, such as allowing land to lie fallow, but the prohibition against wearing cloth of both linen and wool together no longer is reasonable for today because it probably refers to linen being part of the plant world and wool being part of the animal world.

Does all this mean I don't take the Bible literally? Even the most committed fundalits seldom keep the slaves they are supposed to be kind to. It's been a long time since our priests dabbed their earlobes with blood. We look to the Bible for truth, not for laws and legalism—except the universal law of love which transcends all other laws. I love the Bible but I do not want to idolize it, any more than I want to idolize my faith.

Faith can be a very dangerous idol. Am I proud of my faith? Does it separate me, making me feel superior to the rest of Creation? Do I feel that it is my duty to defend my faith against any faith that may in any way be different from my faith? Do I feel that one of the responsibilities of my faith is to protect God from lesser, or other, faiths? Do I need to guard Jesus? Or Christ? Does God need my protection? Is my faith so flimsy that I am fearful for it?

If the answer is yes to any of these questions, then my faith is not iconic. It may not yet have slipped into idolatry, but I had better beware.

During the fifties and sixties parents and teachers were not supposed to discuss Communism with our children in case they got tempted by Marxism. But how were they to know the dangers of Marxism if they did not know anything about it? Today we are not supposed to discuss Buddhism or Hinduism in case our children get snared by these religions. Are we afraid that these religions are so much more potent than Christianity that they are a real danger? Is Christianity so fragile that we need to be afraid of "New Age-ism"?

Meditation has become a fundalit taboo word, but what else was Jesus doing but meditating when he went off, away from his disciples and his friends and followers to be with his Father? Why are we afraid that any knowledge of other faiths will destroy or detract from our own? Are we so unsure of the validity and vitality of our own faith that we are afraid it is weaker than other faiths?

Part of what has nourished my Judeo-Christian faith is, of course, the Bible, and the Bible is a potent icon for me. My parents were Bible readers. I grew up with Bible stories in a big book one of my godparents had given me and which I read over and over again.

When I was in college and that great teacher Mary Ellen Chase told us that anyone seriously interested in writing had to know the King James translation of the Bible intimately because it is the foundation stone of the English language, I took her seriously. I returned to the Bible and I have stayed with it—for all kinds of reasons, both literary and theological. Although I travel with my old, familiar King James translation, I also read many other translations. When my children were little they were far more attracted by J. B. Phillips' contemporary phrases than they were by the sonorous rhythms of the King James. If I had young children now I would read to them from Eugene Petersen's vivid translation of the New Testament, *The Message*. And now I understand, alas, that Peterson is being criticized by the fundalits for his translation because he is "too soft on sin." Is he? Not unless the Bible is.

The Bible is not static. Every time I read it (and I read it daily, so that I have read through all of Scripture many times), it shows me something new and unexpected. This year, when there have been so many terrible ethnic wars plaguing our planet, the violence of the belief in the tribal god (in Deuteronomy, for instance) who wants us to kill all the heathen who worship other gods has struck me forcibly. The Promised Land was land that was already inhabited. The inhabitants were non-Jews, and the land was their home. Those heathen had to be removed, killed, so god's people could take over the land. The use of lowercase there is intentional, advertant.

I have to be willing for the Bible to push me and change me, and I have to read it in the context of the times in which it was written, or it will become an idol, and bibliolotry is as much an idolatry as any other. When we worship what the Bible says and use it as an excuse to be judgmental about those who may respond to a certain passage a little differently from the way we do, that is bibliolotry. If we truly took *all of* the Bible literally we would have to change our eating habits, our clothing habits, our attitudes towards each other. Our priests would have to make regular animal sacrifices, plus wave offerings and heave offerings. Recently my reading has once again taken me through Proverbs, and I was struck anew by the fact that the writer voices two extremes in his attitude towards women: Wisdom is feminine, and wonderful. Women, except for an occasional faithful housewife, are whores, filthy, degraded and degrading. There is some wonderful advice in Proverbs, and some terrible advice, and God help us if we take it all with equal literalness! Child abuse has often been justified by Proverbs: "Spare the rod and spoil the child . . . "

Solomon himself, the supposed author of Proverbs, had even more wives and concubines than his father, and that was looked on with admiration, whereas on the throne of England or in the White House such polygamy and concupiscence would be a scandal—it *is* a scandal. Times change. Mores change. Sometimes for the better, sometimes for the worse; we don't always know which, and so we sometimes choose unwisely.

But the Bible, read as the Word of God, rather than the words of God written by a heavenly scribe as God dictated them, is a delight. (*Shouldn't* the Word of God be a delight?) The Bible is a holy anthology written over thousands of years by poets, historians, dramatists, theologians—a magnificent book spanning many ages. Certain portions of the Bible are truly iconic for me, often the more poetic or the wild and wondrous words in Ezekiel or Daniel or Job. They are open doors to the glory of God, the God who loves and cares for us creatures who still hold the taint of a primordial wrongness.

There are other stories which make my blood run cold, such as the one in Judges where the raped concubine is cut into twelve pieces, each one of which is sent to one of the tribes of Israel. And there are stories which make me laugh with delight, such as Jesus' parable of the importunate woman and the worldly judge. And there are stories which remind me of several of my friends, and of myself, such as the parable of the father who asked his two sons to go do some work for him in his vineyard. The eldest said, "Of course, father," and did not go. The younger said, "I won't!" and then went and did the work his father had asked him to do.

I am not comfortable with the casual way in which Solomon, thought to be so wise, casually slaughtered anybody who might be threatening his throne.

I am comforted by David's desire to repent when he had done wrong, and his ability to speak his whole heart to the Creator.

I am unhappy with Jepthah having to offer his only daughter as a sacrifice to God in order to keep his promise. Maybe a tribal god would appreciate that sacrifice. But the God of love?

I am comforted by Jesus' love for and friendship with Mary of Magdala, and Mary and Martha of Bethany.

Often when I teach a writer's workshop I have the students write stories from Scripture, and I have received some wonderful work from these assignments. I am startled by the number of students, deeply committed Christian young people, who do not know the Bible well and who discover it with joy for the first time. I am awed by those who are not sure that it is permissible to write stories inspired by the Bible but discover that doing so deepens their love and understanding of Scripture. I am delighted by the richness of imagination as it is freed to listen to what God may have to say to us through the great truths found in the pages of Scripture.

One writing assignment which has proven productive is to take any protagonist in Hebrew Scriptures at a time of conflict and decision and write a *midrash* about this person. A midrash is a story which explicates a portion of Scripture, usually an ambiguous or difficult Scripture story.

Often the assignment which follows is for each writer to pass hes or hir (we can get pretty silly about inclusive pronouns) story to the person on the left, and that person is to rewrite the story from the point of view of someone else in the story. We don't often think about how Bildad the Shuhite might have felt, or Leah's or Rachel's maids. What about Cain's wife? What about Lot's wife, or even Jezebel?

Usually when I give an assignment I say, "No less than two pages, no more than five," because I have to read them, and I'm only an ordinary human being with elderly, tired eyes. I also say, "You may not spend more than half an hour on this assignment. The only possible way you can fail is not to try to do it. Listen to your story, and if you're not done in half an hour, that's all right. Let it go." Having a time limit is amazingly freeing, because I have also insisted, "When you write, don't think. Write. Think before you write your story but when you actually sit down to write, listen, don't think. Listen. God and your story may surprise you." And this often happens. Someone will say, "But I didn't expect anyone to pay attention to Jonah, much less the king of Ninevah!" "I didn't think Judah would admit so quickly that he was wrong with Tamar." "I didn't realize how powerful a woman Miriam was!" "Isn't it interesting that so many women didn't have any names, but the midwives who delivered Moses did." I, too, learn from the insights that come from these stories.

An assignment which has had some lovely results is to take any of Jesus' parables and rewrite it for the 1990s. Does the jump of two thousand years change its meaning? Or is the truth Jesus is calling us to still potent today?

Another assignment is to take a sentence from the psalms, or one of the Gospels, and write a half-page journal entry about what this sentence means right now, in your own life. For instance, the first line of Psalm 11: "Blessed is the man that feareth the Lord; he hath great delight in his commandments." Forget, for the moment, the use of "man" and "he" and "his." Remember that *man* is a generic word, meaning both male and female. Read the words with ourselves in mind: "Blessed are we who fear the Lord; we will have great delight in God's commandments." What kind of fear is the psalmist talking about? What kind of fear leads to delight? Not cringing, demeaning fear. Awe, perhaps. Amazement at the wonder of a star trembling into being in a darkening sky. Wonder at the greeting of a friend: "Oh, it's you! I'm so glad to see you!" Marvel at the love surrounding a single dinner table as we hold hands for the blessing of the gathering and the food. That kind of "fear" causes us to desire with our whole heart to keep God's commandments, for they are there for our delight.

It is amazing when I read the "psalms for the day" how a single line will stand out and demand that I pay it particular attention. Some of the psalms I struggle with, such as the last verse of Psalm 137, "By the waters of Babylon we sat down and wept when we remembered Zion. . . . Blessed is he who takes your children and dashes them against the stones." We cringe at that. At least I do. But the singers of that hymn were exiles, strangers in a strange land, and they had seen their own children dashed against the stones. Their law called for revenge—an eye for an eye and a tooth for a tooth. Few of us in America today have any personal understanding of what it means to be brutally forced out of our homes, raped, thrust into hostile enemy territory.

One morning during our adult education class at my church we were discussing the last line of this psalm, and one man whom I know to be honest, honourable, devoted to his Christian faith, brought me up short by telling us that we had missed the point of that verse, which is that God has promised to kill all our enemies and he will do so.

How does one respond to that vindictive, punishing god? I am at a loss for any words of response that would make sense to someone who sees God in terms of wrath and vengeance. Does this man know himself to be loved? I don't think so. I think that he believes that he has succeeded in satisfying God's demands, but that's a very different thing from knowing that we are loved. I don't believe that I, with all my faults and flaws, can ever succeed in satisfying God's demands. Always I fall short. And yet I know myself to be loved by the loving God who made me—and everybody and everything else there is. We fail God's love constantly; we must grieve God deeply; and yet I believe that God loves us utterly, loves us enough to "send his only begotten son."

So we continue to try to learn about God's love, and the psalms, those ancient, powerful hymns, are there to help us.

I have wrestled with many of the parables, as well as the psalms, but often because I have tried to take them as things-in-themselves and forgotten the point Jesus was making in telling them; often his point was our human hardness of heart. We forget, too, where the parables come in the chronology of Jesus' life.

I am coming to see that when we take Jesus' stories out of their chronological place in his life we can easily misunderstand him. In one of the many vineyard stories, the owner is away and sends servants to collect his rent and his dues, and the workers kill the servant. The owner sends more servants, and they, too, are stoned and killed. This happens several times, and finally the owner sends his only son, thinking that he will be treated with respect, but the workers kill the son, too. It's an ugly story, but it makes a lot of sense if we put it in its proper chronology. It is towards the end of Jesus' life, and he is telling the story to the very people he knows are planning to kill him. It is a pointed story, and not one he told early on in his mission. It is dangerous to take it out of context.

Over and over I have unhappily contemplated the story of the blasted fig tree, a story in the life of Jesus which has always left me with many questions. A year ago, I heard a monk tell about a woman whose brilliant daughter was manic-depressive. The daughter struggled with her affliction, but ultimately she committed suicide. The mother asked the monk to preach at the funeral. She said, "I don't want to hear about the Resurrection and heaven or anything like that. I want you to preach about the blasted fig tree." It is understandable that the woman saw a metaphor for her daughter in the blasted fig tree.

Jesus wanted the fig tree to give him some cooling figs, but it was barren of fruit because it was not the season for the fig tree to bear fruit, so he blasted it.

That is not an affirmative story. I don't like it. I have never liked it. I can see why that woman wanted the monk to preach about it at her daughter's funeral. Those who die by suicide were, not so long ago, forbidden funerals and burial in consecrated ground. Mostly we no longer put that judgment on them. The monk did not tell us what he said in the sermon; I wish he had.

So once again I struggled with the blasted fig tree.

I used to think there were only two possible explanations. One was that the incident never happened. The Gospels were written long after Jesus' death. This story may have come from faulty memory.

The other interpretation I gave this story was that if Jesus said, "Bear fruit," you would be given the ability to do so. When he said, "Take up your bed and walk," the afflicted man was cured and able to do what Jesus commanded. So why didn't the tree bear fruit? That is the tough question.

A third possibility came to me this past Holy Week. Timing. We often take the stories of or about Jesus out of context, and so, out of time. When did he blast the fig tree? During what we call Holy Week. Palm Sunday had come and gone, The cries of, "Hosannah in the highest! Blessed is he who comes in the name of the Lord!" were no more than faint echoes. It did not take supernatural knowledge for Jesus to anticipate that the cries of praise would change to cries of "Crucify him! Crucify him!" He knew that mobs are fickle. He knew that mobs feed on and enjoy hate. His disciples were unwilling to accept it when he told them that he was going to have to die. Nobody understood.

One preacher said that when Jesus was crucified, he knew that his mission was accomplished, that he had succeeded in what he came to do. I am not sure about that preacher's statement. Did the mortal Jesus feel that he had accomplished what he had come for, or did he, at least for a terrible moment in his humanness, feel that he had failed?

Certainly, in human, secular terms, he was a failure, and not even a spectacular failure, just one more Jew who got in trouble with the authorities and was crucified for it; his death on the cross wasn't anything unusual.

It was a dark week, that week that was ultimately to be called Holy Week. For Jesus it must have held a terrible realization that he was not understood, not even by his closest friends. He knew the painful loneliness caused by that woeful lack of understanding. He knew that those who hated him and wanted him dead were going to have their own way and that death would be neither quick nor easy.

Perhaps the human Jesus, in his loneliness and anguish, lashed out at the fig tree.

Someone has suggested that perhaps Jesus saw himself as that fig tree, unable to bear fruit out of season. What a terrible thought, but it shouldn't be pushed aside as impossible.

We will never know why Jesus cursed that fig tree. Not in this life. We are not able, with our finite minds, to comprehend that Jesus was mortal and immortal, human and divine. It is too much. But if I accept Jesus' humanity as well as his divinity, then I must allow the human Jesus to do things I don't like. The Incarnation does mean that God was willing to become mortal for the sake of us mortal creatures, that Infinite Power and Love willingly and lovingly went through every temptation that comes to any one of us. It is a love so astonishing that it can only be rejoiced in, lived by, but never understood.

Jesus told another story about a fig tree that was not bearing fruit. The owner felt that the fig tree was useless and should be cut down. But the gardener suggested that he tend the fig tree, cultivate it, fertilize it, and then, if it still did not bear fruit, cut it down.

I like that story better, but it doesn't mean I don't struggle with the stricken fig tree. I have struggled with the workers in the vineyard who were all paid the same wages, though many of them had worked all day in the heat of the sun, and a few only in the coolness of the last hour. But I am learning that it is a story about Grace, rather than fair labor practices.

All of the stories that Jesus told reveal their deepest meaning if we see them in their chronological context.

I remember yet again that Jesus told stories—stories which were not intended to be literal, but which were to make a point, and I know that my understanding is widened far more by stories than by provable fact. If it's provable, where's the mystery? Where's the faith? What is there to understand?

I am, as ever, grateful that the Scriptural protagonists are not virtuous or moral or perfect, but fallible mortals like the rest of us, struggling to understand what God wants of them, and often getting only the merest glimpse of the purpose for which they have been called.

The man who believed that the last line of "By the waters of Babylon" is God's promise to slaughter all his enemies is a fundamentalist-literalist, a fundalit. Perhaps the opposite of fundalit is permissivist. No matter what has been done, the permissivist finds an excuse. "He really needed to fulfill himself; that was more important than . . . " "She really needed to get away, even though her children . . . " Everything we do, no matter what, is all right. We are forgiven.

Yes, oh yes, we are forgiven. But everything is not all right. It is not all right to murder your wife and her lover. It is not all right to desert or drown your children. It is not all right to shoot and kill people in an abortion clinic, no matter how profoundly you believe abortion is murder. One sin does not justify another.

Right now I am struggling to understand a recent suicide. Suicide used to be considered a mortal sin. Some suicides I can understand;

someone with a terminal disease wanting to spare the family from having to watch, to cope with, all the pain and horror. Someone suffering from depression so dark that no ray of hope can come in. But it is still not all right.

There is a French saying that to understand everything is to forgive everything, and that is true. But if we can understand it, is there any need to forgive it? The things I find hardest to forgive, as well in myself as in others, are the things I do not understand. It's something like faith and proof: we don't need faith for anything we can prove.

We struggle to understand, sometimes beyond reason. I have a friend who berates herself for her lack of understanding, and I cry out, "But if you could understand it all, you'd be God!" I cry that to myself, too. We can understand far more than we do, but complete knowledge and understanding are not for us finite mortals in this life.

It wasn't until I began working on my novel *Certain Women* that I realized how reluctant God was for the Hebrew people to have a king and how everything in their history went downhill after they crowned, and worshipped, a mortal king, even as charismatic a monarch as David.

Every time I read the Bible God gives me a new Word, and I am grateful.

Mostly what it tells and retells me is that God is love, and we are given that love through Grace, not because we deserve it. Thank God, God does not give us what we deserve!

Thank God, God is more ready to forgive than to punish. Thank God Jesus made it quite clear that he had come to be with and to help those in need. "Those who are well do not need a physician," he said, "but those who are ill." Jesus said those are the ones he had come to help. When I am most miserable in mind, body, or spirit, that is when I need God's love the most and reach out for it in the greatest desperation. And even when I do not immediately recognize it, it is always there.

How many of us are like Namaan the leper who thought that dipping himself in the nearby river was too ordinary a thing to do to cure his leprosy and wanted the prophet to suggest something more spectacular! But God over and over again uses the ordinary things of creation: water, earth, fire, air.

In the New Testament the Hebrew Scriptures are frequently referred to, and we are expected to recognize the reference, without having it explained. It is important for us to know the Bible that Jesus knew so thoroughly if we are to understand what is in the New Testament. I also love many of the stories in the Deutero-canonical books—the Apocrypha: Susannah and the Elders, the story of Tobias and the Angel in the book of Tobit, and the fire before the altar in Macabees that burned steadily for a week, although there was only enough oil in it for a few hours. There is always something new, especially at night when I take more time with my readings than I do in the mornings (when I always seem to be in a hurry to get to work on time, to get on with the business of the day).

In the evening I bathe and then sit in my quiet corner with my Prayer Book and Bible. If Barbara, my house mate, is at home, we read Compline together, plus the psalms for the day, sometimes comparing translations, often laughing, occasionally wiping away tears, but deeply together in our quiet worship. Compline is one of the ancient monastic offices, the go-to-bed-quietly office, read sitting down comfortably, so that body and mind can relax before the lights are turned out. It helps clear our minds of the accumulation of the day. Then, in the peace, I can quietly ask myself what I may have done during the day which would grieve God ("tick Jesus off"), and what would have given my Maker pleasure. When we refuse to hate, to look for revenge, to be prideful, but instead, forgive, let go, offer ourselves in love, surely that gives God pleasure. When I am clever at someone else's expense, that does not; when I have tried to serve whatever God has given me that day, I hope that it does. I do want to give pleasure to God! And that means accepting myself, just as I am, without one plea, and my evening readings about God's scriptural people help me here, for they are so like me.

I recently came across an article written by a priest who pronounced that if one does not feel close to God during accident or illness, one's faith is inadequate.

Most certainly our faith is inadequate! It always is! But I wonder how much pain that particular priest had ever suffered? I wonder on what he based such a statement? The healing of my body after that near-fatal accident was a gift; I believed that it was God telling me that there was still work for me to do. I believed, too, that as God healed my body, so my spirit would be healed, and that, too, would be a gift, rather than an act of will or virtue on my part.

Sometimes in our lives occasions come when we are too wounded, either physically or spiritually, to be able to pray, when we feel torn away from God. But we are always part of the body of Christ. I think of the Russian Orthodox Church services which go on for three or four hours—and people stand or walk about, not sit. There are no false expectations that anyone will be able to be focussed on the service all of the time, but the realistic expectation is that *someone* in the congregation will be focussed all of the time, and so the continuity of worship and the rhythm of prayer is not broken.

Before we left for Antarctica I was talking to a preacher friend whose leg had been badly shattered in a fall, and when I told him that after my accident I had not felt close to God, that I had been lost in pain, he looked at me in gratitude and exclaimed, "Oh, thank you!" And we agreed that even when we do not feel close to God, God is close to us. That is part of the mystery: no matter how far we feel from God, God is never far from us, for we bear God's image within us. There have been times when I have felt that when the surgeons opened me up to see how much damage bleeding kidneys and intestines had suffered, when they cut out my spleen, they cut out God, too. When one is in the depths, that kind of thinking is not an unusual temptation, but it is a temptation and needs to be rejected. Simply knowing that it is a temptation is helpful; Satan always attacks when we are weak.

Maybe that's why I love the icon of Jesus with his tongue stuck out! When theologians or scientists postulate that we are the only inhabited planet in the universe, I wonder if the Creator isn't distressed with what we are doing with Love's creation. I can't help thinking that in the vastness of the universe there must be other inhabited planets, perhaps with life forms quite different from ours, who have done better with God's gift of free will than we have. I somehow can't believe that we are the only experiment. Years ago I wrote a science fiction story of exploration of other planets. In one far distant planet where life had become extinct, an ancient volume was found, written in a strange alphabet. When it was finally deciphered, the first sentence began, "In the beginning was the Word . . . "

I don't think that's an original thought with me.

Perhaps the only original thought I can think of is God's thought in Creation, in the Word shouting all the galaxies into being. How awesome! How wondrous! How terrifying!

Twice in the past year I have been asked by someone still young enough not to be afraid to ask the question, "Are you afraid of death?" And I answer, "Yes, of course I am. Death is change, and no matter how deep our faith, change is frightening." But then I have been able to add, "But when I was in an automobile accident and was badly hurt and knew that I was probably dying, I was not afraid." There's the marvel, the unexpected grace. I was not afraid. Before I went under the anesthetic I thanked God for my life, which had already been long and full. "It's been a terrific journey," I said to God. "Thank you." And then the anaesthetic took over. And then, to my surprise, I woke up! Here I was, still on planet earth, and I lay there, believing that since I was still here, God still had work for me to do.

It was a long time before I was strong enough to hold the Bible again, and when I was, I knew that I was truly on the way to being healed. So I read and reread the great book which inspires me to use my imagination, to think, to rejoice in God's forgiveness and grace. It helps me to love myself and my neighbour as it reveals more and more of God's love.

Thank you. Thank you.

12

HELL AND HEAVEN

 It isn't easy to make hell into an icon, but it is horridly easy to make it into an idol, and we do that whenever we consign anybody to hell. I'm not thinking so much of the casual, "Oh, go to hell," though that's bad enough, but of one group deliberately and literally consigning another group to hell.

It is bothersome, to put it mildly, when Christians think they have the right to decide who is going to heaven and who is going to hell. Why should any human being have that right?

What kind of hell are they thinking of?

It often seems to be literal and pre-Copernican, heaven above, with golden harps and pink clouds, and hell below, full of burning pitch and everlasting flames and little red devils with pitchforks. How can anyone who believes in God's love *want* anyone to be in such eternal torture? It makes me cold with pain.

I do not know what heaven is like, neither do I know what hell is like. I do believe that most of us still have a lot to learn, and for Tiberius, Hitler, drug dealers and pushers, terrorists, that learning is going to be terrible indeed, for what we all have to learn is love. Maybe it's more like going back to square one than burning pitch.

And what about the Lord of Love whom I have tried all my life to affirm? We all see God in our own way, closer to some people than others in our vision of God. I do not see "my" God the way the fundalits see their punitive God. Nor do I see "my" God the same God as the God of those who depend on intellectual proof for their belief, or the bland God of the permissivists. "My" God is not the same as the God of those who believe that Jesus had to come to save us from an angry Father, those who believe that God will kill all their enemies. Different Gods? In a sense, yes.

Where—who—is the One True God? Beyond all our attempts at comprehension. Not one of us completely understands the nature of God. That is why all our attempts at understanding have at least a tinge of our own anthropomorphism. When I say "my God" I am not being blasphemous or polytheistic. I love, trust, worship "my" God, and "my" simply means my own fumbling, fallible, faltering definition of God Who is One, Who is All.

During a question-and-answer session a woman once asked about a passage from John's Gospel: What about Jesus being the only way? And I realized that she was asking the question in the hope of receiving an exclusive, not an inclusive answer. I replied, "For me, Jesus is the way, the truth, the life, but as for the rest of the world, I am quite happy to leave it to God. It is not my prerogative to make such judgments. It is God's." But she, and most of the others who ask that question, don't really want to know whether or not Jesus is the way for me. They want to know that those who do not accept Jesus as the way are damned. They are more interested in the damnation than the salvation of two-thirds of the world. As I read and reread the first chapters of Genesis, damnation was not in the Creator's agenda! Creation, not damnation. Salvation, not damnation. Love, not damnation. When Jesus spoke those words recorded in John, he accepted the geographic and philosophical boundaries of the Jews of two thousand years ago, who struggled to live in an occupied country under the domination of secular Rome.

Am I being a permissivist, here? I don't think so. We *can* refuse heaven. Is an atheist (often someone who can't believe in God because there's no reconciling a God of love with a planet of woe) further from heaven than a fundalit? I just don't believe that God will ever give up on any part of creation, not with the drug pusher, or those of other religions, or fundalits, or permissivists, or you, or me.

Why do we hang on to our old human ideas and so turn them into idols? We have hardly changed our view of the universe since the discoveries of Galileo and Copernicus; we still worry that the discoveries of science may discredit God, as though God is as finite and flawed as we are. It would have been natural for our visualizations of heaven and hell to have changed with the discoveries of the billions of galaxies that surround us, and the equal billions of subatomic particles in the world of the microcosm, and it is amazing to me that they haven't, at least not for a lot of people. And not only Christians. "Teeth will be provided!"

Since the bombing of the twin towers of the World Trade Center in downtown Manhattan, of the federal building in Oklahoma City, there has been a lot of awareness of terrorists of all kinds. Did the gun-loving bombers in Oklahoma believe they were saving civilization? Does an Islamic terrorist see bombing a plane as an act of virtue which will send the terrorist directly to heaven, while those he has killed will go to hell? Is that truly very different from the Christian legalist who wants a lot of people in hell in order to feel saved and superior?

I would not want to spend eternity with the self-satisfied souls who think they deserve heaven, while everybody else belongs in hell. I'd rather be in hell with Gandhi and Teilhard de Chardin and George MacDonald and all the innocent people who've been killed by terrorist bombs, than in heaven with the self-proclaimed virtuous. But aren't they really in hell? Can I damn another fellow being without tasting hell myself? Can I hate other Christians without plunging my own heart into hell? When I am judgmental I am opening the gates of hell.

I make my own hell when I want too much to belong, to be part of the group or the inner circle, to be, as Carson McCullers put it, "a member of the wedding." I still have the longing of the little girl on the outside who wanted to be in the secret club. But if I have to be a literalist or a legalist to do so, if I have to believe that hell is going to be heavily populated with all the "others," then I can no more join the club than I could as the ten-year-old camper who refused to take the final step of the initiation into the little girls' club.

It is, to me, as repellent as that. Indeed, it is blasphemous. How dare we claim God's prerogative and decide who is going to heaven and who to hell? Is that not totally self-centered pride? To be caught up in one's own self-righteousness would be a terrible punishment indeed. My friend Tallis once remarked that hell would be having your own way all of the time.

I know that in my own life when I am self-centered, I am in hell. And when I am most thrown out of myself in delight or joy or love, then I have a foretaste of heaven. I do not know, in any literalistic way, what either heaven or hell will *look* like, and I very much doubt if they are going to be like the medieval illustrations, but I do have a sense of what they may *be* like.

One night in North Carolina, after I had given two major talks, autographed (literally) hundreds of books and had stood up, ready to leave after the final reception, a woman in distress came up to me, asking, "Can you explain things like my son-in-law's death at thirty-five?"

Heavily I sat down. "No. I can't explain it. These things happen, and sometimes they happen because of abuse of our own free will, and sometimes they happen as the result of our polluted planet, and sometimes they are completely unexplainable. All I know is that they matter to God, and that God can come into them and help us to bear them, and perhaps even become stronger because of it."

The woman said, "I was told that he died because God wanted him in heaven."

I shook my head. I had no answer to that, either, except that it didn't make much sense to me, as it obviously made no sense to her. We grasp at straws, and always have, trying to explain the unexplainable. We talked a little longer, and again I stood up to leave. A small group of women approached me. "What about evil? In your talks you seem to indicate that there is evil outside the evil that we do."

I sat down again. I explained that philosophers and theologians have been trying to explain the problem of evil for millennia, that hundreds of books have been written about it, and I was certainly not going to try to explain it, ever, and particularly not at the tag end of a very long day.

But they persisted. "You do believe there are evil powers?" Yes. Yes, I do. So did Paul. Principalities, thrones, dominions, and powers. Some good. Some fallen. Good angels and evil angels. Paul believed in them, but he did not explain them. Neither can I, though I have to admit that I believe in them, and I also have to emphasize that no matter how strong they are this does not let us off the hook of free will, or the consequences of our own actions.

In their tempting us the fallen angels are plausible and mimic good. If they were easy to recognize, like the demons in some "Christian" novels, we would have little trouble from them; they would be resistible. But they tickle our vanity; they work on our low estimations of ourselves and make us feel better. They assure us we have a right to join any club we want to. We can even be president of it. They pat us on the back and praise us. It is not a bad thing to have honest praise for work well done. The problem is when we take the praise to ourselves as though we deserve it.

But—don't we? Yes. And no. When I do a good job I know that I have not done it alone. The good, the holy angels have been with me. The Holy Spirit has been part of it. Don't ask me to explain it. Inspiration cannot be explained. When we are *in-spired* (in-spirited) we are awed, we are grateful. But it is too mysterious to be explained.

But what about the evil spirits? Is it always our "fault" when we heed them? I heard a sermon in which the preacher said that to believe in evil spirits is to find excuses for our own evil behaviour. "I couldn't help it. Satan made me do it." Satan can not "make us do it"! The preacher was right in that we often try to find excuses for our own misbehaviour ("out came this calf," as Aaron said), and blaming our sin on Satan or other evil spirits is an easy way out. But that's not all of it. The fallen angels cannot *make* us obey their ugly suggestions. We are creatures with free will, and we can say, "No, I won't do that. That is wrong. That is not loving."

But what about evil—small children kidnapped and sold into prostitution? What about the abuse of the little ones? That is one of the most terrible of all evils, and surely the holy angels must long to heal, comfort, protect, even if they have to wait until after death.

Do we always know what is wrong and what is right? Values change with the centuries and with society. For how many centuries did we accept slavery? In Victorian days it was "wrong" to say *please* or *thank you* to the servants, and it was "wrong" for doctors to give women in labour anything to ease the pains of childbirth, because the Bible predicts that women will give birth in pain. Today, common courtesy demands that we say *please* and *thank you* to anyone who has done us a service, and childbirth is seen as honourable, even glorious, and we thank God for pain relief. How do we know right from wrong? Alas, we don't, not all the time. The only law to guide us is the law of love, and that transcends cultural differences.

But does that really address the question: Is there evil outside us?

I believe that there is, though like the preacher I am leery of anyone saying, "The devil made me do it." I'm also leery of people who say, "God made me do it," usually after some strange or dreadful action. God does not coerce, or take away that extraordinary gift of will, part of which includes the power to resist.

But there is also evil over which we have no power, unexplainable accidents, horrors, evil events.

A truck driver ran carelessly through a red light, bashed in the little car in which I was being driven (with the completed manuscript of *Certain Women* in its red box on the back seat), and nearly killed me. Often it's the passive person in the passenger seat who gets killed. A tornado slashes through a village of mobile homes and kills half the residents. A child is caught in the crossfire of bullets meant for someone else.

But is there also deliberate evil that does not stem from anything we can identify and point at? I believe that there is, that the war in heaven continues and is reflected in the wars on earth. Evil feeds on greed—what a horror of greed is the growing and selling of drugs in order to make money out of peoples' weakness and dependency. There are mobs heedlessly trampling people to death. My husband was once caught in a mob, and he said that it had a personality of its own, quite aside from that of any individual person who was part of the mob.

I also believe that if the powers of evil are active in the universe, so are the powers of good. "Where evil is, there does grace abound." And I believe that consistently we need to look for good, and not for evil, that when we look for evil we call up evil, while heaven comes closer when we ackowledge it.

But if my hope of heaven depends on someone else's damnation, am I not excluding myself from heaven? And am I not trivializing the prayer, "Forgive us our trespasses as we forgive those who trespass against us?" Jesus is firm that as we forgive, so we shall be forgiven. He is also firm that we must not judge; otherwise we shall be judged.

It is, once again, fear that causes the negative question which looks for the negative answer. During the question-and-answer sessions after I speak there are many more positive questions than negative ones, and many of these deal with deep and unanswerable problems, problems which can be faced only because we believe God's love is stronger than any of the powers of hell.

The question about evil is asked more and more regularly. The second question which has increased in the last year is "Why do you stay in the established church?" And I reply, "Some of us have to hang in there." And, "We can't change it from outside." And, "I don't believe we can be Christians in isolation. We need community." There's a lot about my church (as with most churches) that I don't like, as well as a lot that I like, and it is the community of like-minded people I have found there that keeps me faithful. Whenever I bump into fear and judgmentalism in the congregation and respond with defensiveness I am given a foretaste of hell. Whenever I meet with love and tender prayer and deep compassion I am given a foretaste of heaven.

In the late summer I went to speak at the Charles River Arts Festival on the last weekend of a wonderful summer program for children from eight to fifteen, during which they may sign up for any kind of art class they want (writing, painting, dancing, etc.). There is a loving and permissive atmosphere in the camp. But the arts themselves demand such committed discipline that this group of well over a hundred kids was one of the best-disciplined groups I had ever encountered. When I went to the girls' washroom, it was clean and tidy.

And I was reminded of going to Tulsa, Oklahoma, with my husband, for his fiftieth high school graduation reunion. We were taken to the brand new Tulsa Central High, and when a few of us went to the girls' bathroom it was already trashed. The doors had been yanked off the cubicles. The wash basins were cracked or actually pulled out from the walls.

And I wondered: Why? What's the difference?

And I thought: Those kids at Charles River are proud of themselves. They honour themselves, and so they honour their surroundings. What can we do in the public school system to make young people proud of themselves? Where has this self-respect gone? When Hugh was at Tulsa Central High the washrooms were not trashed. Aren't the kids who are wrecking their surroundings creating a hell of their own? Conversely, those students at Charles River were preparing themselves for heaven. We will recognize neither heaven nor hell after we die unless we prepare ourselves now.

When I go on a speaking engagement in a specifically Christian setting, I and the people I meet can jump a lot of the usual superficial chit chat and move directly into important issues. We are free, because of our shared faith, to be vulnerable with each other. In October I had a wonderful time at St. Thomas More College in Saskatoon, Saskatchewan. Saskatoon is a town on a river, and there is more sky there than I have ever seen, even in Nebraska! It sweeps uninterruptedly from horizon to horizon. Already the trees were stripped of leaves. There were snow flurries. At the time of the turning of leaves at home it was already winter in Saskatoon. I was told that in mid-winter the temperature can reach forty below, and at forty below Fahrenheit and Celsius converge.

One evening at dinner the owner of the local bookstore told us about his father in Odessa at the time of the Russian Revolution. His father was seven, and his Mennonite family had settled in Odessa when they fled Germany and went into Russia to escape religious persecution. With the revolution the persecution jumped the border and became slaughter. The women were raped. The men were shot. The seven-year-old boy saw his father felled by a bullet.

I asked, "Have you written about this?"

No. He had not. Several of us urged him to do so, because we felt that the story should not be forgotten.

He was not sure. He talked about how the North American Indian elders are very slow to trust anybody with their stories or their knowledge. And with cause. For instance, the Indians have a root which is an effective heart medicine; when the white men heard about it they dug it up and sold it at exorbitant prices, without knowing anything about how it worked or how it should be used, thereby destroying the *vertue* in it. Many incidents like that have made the Indians reluctant to tell their stories, because they are rightly afraid that the stories will be distorted. Yes, they will be, I agreed. But, I reminded him, if the story is not told, it dies.

Yes, if it is told it is changed, abused, it deteriorates. Isn't that what has happened with Christianity? How close are any of our varied Christian stories to the original? How far have we strayed from the Gospel?

How far are our Christian denominations and sects from the oneness of early Christianity?

Any group which tries to recover the original Christian love and freedom is hunted, killed, tortured by the dominant Christian establishment, or by the establishment that feels it ought to be dominant and is lashing out in anger and fear.

So, do we lose the story? Or do we keep telling it, even knowing that it is going to be distorted and mutilated? I believe that we must go on telling it, in whatever way we can, knowing that we cannot do it justice. If we fool ourselves into thinking that we have it right, we are in trouble. We tend to defend vigorously things that in our deepest hearts we are not quite certain about. If we are certain of something we know, it doesn't need defending! If we feel that we have to defend God, aren't we displaying a powerless god, unable to defend Love's own creation?

Walter Brueggeman writes in *Texts under Negotiation,* "Our ego-structure is possible only because we censor and select in the same way . . . we have had to censor and select texts." We've done it in the lectionary, "And when these censored parts surface, they are dangerously subversive."

In real life we all censor and select in some way in order to keep our sanity. It is normal, even necessary. But there is a line, which is too often crossed, past which it becomes abnormal and destructive. When we censor out most of the world in order to protect our own little version of it, we are creating a kind of hell. Brueggeman says, "We also have had our horizon bounded by 'the possible,' when our lives in the Gospel are framed only by the impossible."

When we are able to accept the astounding impossible love in the Gospel, then we are experiencing a foretaste of heaven.

The Churches have tended to be too literal about heaven and hell, defining what no mortal can possibly know, because only God knows. A young woman came to me, deeply disturbed, because her minister had told her that immortality is not a Christian concept. It is left over from Greek thinking, he said, and Christians are not supposed to believe in it.

This was not what she needed to hear. She had lost a beloved sister, and she needed affirmation, not a lecture. "If there is no immortality, then what about my sister?" she asked the minister.

"We believe in the resurrection of the body," he said. "What body?" Her sister had died, very slowly, of cancer, looking like a victim from Belsen. Her sister would not want to be resurrected in that emaciated, dying body. Her minister did not have an answer, at least not one that she could remember and tell me.

"I think," I said slowly, "that the word *immortality* involves time, involves our going on and on in time, human time. But resurrection is in eternity, and that's a tough concept for us to understand."

"Do you understand it?"

"No. but I believe it. I don't understand it because I am in time right now. I get glimpses of eternity, of *kairos*, God's time, which is far more wonderful than ordinary *chronos*, clock time."

"What about my sister? She was so alive, so vibrant, until those last months."

All I could do was repeat my affirmation that God does not create us and then drop us into nothingness. I don't think her sister is in either the old-fashioned heaven or hell; but I think she is, somehow, somewhere, more truly alive than she was on earth. I don't know what the resurrection body will be like.

Tommy, my evangelist friend, quoted something to the effect that many Christians are more interested in resuscitation than resurrection.

Ouch.

My grandfather would not have wished to be resuscitated at age 101.

But when a child is suddenly killed, don't we intuitively wish for resuscitation? We want that child back, exactly as before—the same deep gray eyes, the fair hair, the dimples that came and went.

But Jesus was never recognized by sight after the resurrection. So what on earth do we mean by resurrection?

When the people asked St. Paul what the resurrection body was going to be like, he snapped out, "Don't be silly," one of my favourites of all the sayings of Paul. Don't be silly. We can't have back what we have lost. I can't have my tall, lean husband with his amazing blue eyes, larger and bluer than any other eyes I have seen.

I want him back, there's no evading that I want him.

So what do I mean, what do we all mean when we say that "we believe in the resurrection of the dead"?

A friend said to me, "When I die and see Jack again I will recognize him."

If we didn't recognize Jesus, can we count on that? Not unless we, too, have been resurrected, not resuscitated.

Once again we are in mystery, outside the realm of provable fact. We are, I believe, given glimpses, and I have had a few. Walking down a dirt road on a shining summer day I moved into a realm of beauty and depth that became indescribable once I had left it, but it gives me a hint that after I die I may say, "Oh, glory! What a thin way of living I have just left!"

I don't know what heaven is like, or hell, because as they are presented to us they are largely human constructs. My affirmation, which has always been my affirmation, is that Love does not create and then abandon or annihilate, and that our risen bodies will be shaped according to God's original pattern. Once again we are in the cloud of unknowing, where our belief is far more profound than our knowledge.

Wherever there is love, heaven is being experienced. Whenever we are lost in hate, we are in hell, no matter how Christian we think we are. We often fool ourselves, and that is a matter for pleasure among the echthroi, the fallen angels, the haters, the annihilators. But we can, with prayer and openness, fool ourselves less and love more. When I read Evening or Morning Prayer with a friend I am helped, even more than when I am alone, to open myself to God's love. My response is never adequate, just as no human description of God is ever adequate, but God's blessings are more abundant than we often realize. I held a beautiful baby in my arms at the time of her baptism: the joy of that ceremony was another foretaste of heaven. When I hold hands with the women in my study group at the end of our time together, and we pray for each other, for those we know who are in need of prayer, for the whole world, that, too, is a foretaste of heaven. So is lighting the candles for a meal I have prepared for family or friends. These are the times when I am freed from self-centeredness and contained in God's love. Isn't that, in a way, practise for life after death?

That is enough. We are in trouble, if not in hell, when we attempt to define the undefinable.

Another minister, of a similar mindset to the one who said *immortality* is not a Christian concept, announced that *soul* is not a Christian concept, but another leftover from the Greeks.

Yet we need the word *soul*, a word to express our ousia, our essence. My *me* is far more than my seventy-five-year-old body. My *me* is not any age at all, is in *kairos* rather than in *chronos*. *Soul* may come from the Greek, but it is as good a word as any.

When I die, my body will go, probably into the (earthly) flames, since cremation seems the simplest way on this overcrowded planet where there is no longer space for quiet and spacious graveyards.

But what about my *me*, my soul, that spark which enlivens my body? What about my husband, parents, friends, all those who have gone before me? Does death have the last word? If immortality and soul are not Christian concepts, what, then, is our theology of Resurrection?

Again, we are in mystery, and discussions of the Greek-ness of immortality or soul are no more than ways of avoiding the mystery, of denying our need for icons. In Russia there are many icons of the death of Mary, the Theotokos, and a joyful affirmation of her empty tomb. Affirmation, not explanation.

O God, my God, if I believe in you at all, I must believe in you all the way, in my birth, my life, my death, and, ultimately, into your love.

Into your love.

That love which is heaven.

Amen.

Books in the **Wheaton Literary Series:**

And It was Good: Reflections on Beginnings, by Madeleine L'Engle. Cloth, 213 pages.

At a Theater Near You: Screen Entertainment from a Christian Perpective, by Thomas Patterson. Trade paper, 216 pages.

A Cry Like a Bell, poems by Madeleine L'Engle. Trade paper, 110 pages.

The Heart of George MacDonald: A One-Volume Collection of His Most Important Fiction, Essays, Sermons, Drama, and Biographical Information, edited by Roland Hein. Cloth, 448 pages.

How to Read Slowly: Reading for Comprehension, by James W. Sire. Trade paper, 192 pages.

The Liberated Imagination: Thinking Christianly about the Arts, by Leland Ryken. Trade paper, 283 pages.

Life Essential: The Hope of the Gospel, by George MacDonald, edited by Roland Hein. Trade paper, 104 pages.

Maker & Craftsman: The Story of Dorothy L. Sayers, by Alzina Stone Dale. Trade paper, 172 pages.

Odd Angles of Heaven: Contemporary Poetry by People of Faith, edited by David Craig and Janet McCann. Cloth, 160 pages.

Orthodoxy, by G. K. Chesterton. Cloth, 192 pages.

Penguins and Golden Calves: Icons and Idols by Madeleine L'Engle. Cloth, 192 pages.

Polishing the Petosky Stone, poems by Luci Shaw (compiled from **Listen to the Green, The Secret Trees, The Sighting,** and **Postcard from the Shore).** Cloth, 288 pages.

Postcard from the Shore, poems by Luci Shaw. Trade paper, 95 pages.

Realms of Gold: The Classics in Christian Perspective, by Leland Ryken. Trade paper, 240 pages.

The Rock that Is Higher: Story as Truth, by Madeleine L'Engle. Cloth, 304 pages.

The Sighting, poems by Luci Shaw. Trade paper, 95 pages.

Sold into Egypt: Joseph's Journey into Human Being, by Madeleine L'Engle. Cloth, 240 pages.

A Stone for a Pillow: Journeys with Jacob, by Madeleine L'Engle. Cloth, 213 pages.

T. S. Eliot: The Philosopher Poet, by Alzina Stone Dale. Cloth, 209 pages.

Walking on Water: Reflections on Faith and Art, by Madeleine L'Engle. Trade paper, 198 pages.

The Weather of the Heart, poems by Madeleine L'Engle. Trade paper, 96 pages.

All available from your local bookstore or from Harold Shaw Publishers, Box 567, Wheaton, IL 60189. 1-800-SHAWPUB